Playing with Words

Playing with Words

Humour in the English language

Barry J. Blake

LONDON   OAKVILLE

First published in 2007

UK: Equinox Publishing Ltd, Unit 6, The Village, 101 Amies Street,
London SW11 2JW
US: DBBC, 28 Main Street, Oakville, CT 06779
www.equinoxpub.com

The author thanks Everyman's Library, an imprint of Alfred A. Knopf,
for permission to quote 'The Cow', by Ogden Nash, from *Collected
Verse, from 1929 On.* © 1961.

British Library Cataloguing-in-Publication Data
A catalogue record for this book is available from the British Library.

ISBN-13   978 1 84553 330 4 (paperback)

Library of Congress Cataloging-in-Publication Data
Blake, Barry J.
Playing with words : humour in the English language / Barry J. Blake.
    p. cm.
Includes bibliographical references and index.
ISBN-13: 978-1-84553-330-4 (pb)
1. Wit and humor—History and criticism. 2. Play on words. I. Title.

PN6147.B53 2007
817—dc22

                                        2006101427

Typeset by S.J.I. Services, New Delhi
Printed and bound in Great Britain by Lightning Source UK Ltd,
Milton Keynes, and Lightning Source Inc., La Vergne, TN

Contents

Introduction

Language is mostly used for serious business like telling your book-maker that you really meant to back No. 3 in the fifth, not No. 5 in the third, or asking Sister Immaculata if she wants to see *Lust in the Dust*. But language is also a source of amusement. We can use it to be funny, to be witty. We can laugh at ourselves and others making a slip of the tongue or coming out with the wrong word. We can write amusing verses.

Very few people confine themselves to the formal, staid language of the type you might use in speaking to a stranger from another culture. Most people use a lot of colloquialisms for a start, and these are often smart and witty. There is a certain cleverness in words like *butterfingers* or phrases such as *not since Adam was a boy*, though such expressions lose their effectiveness once they are in common use. A majority of people relay jokes. Many use pleasantries and other light-hearted remarks as part of getting along with others. Some make clever jibes with a view to eliciting a clever retort.

Language play is part of normal language use. There are only a few situations where it is excluded. We do not use any form of language play in drafting laws or rules of conduct, for instance, and we don't try to be smart in business letters, at least not in those that the recipient might not want to receive. But these situations are few. Humour can sometimes be found in sermons, for instance, and even at funerals there are often humorous anecdotes and light-hearted remarks in the eulogy.

Humour and other types of word play form a bigger part of our normal experience of language than most people probably recognize. Consider a typical young couple, Debbie and Mark. They start the day listening to a breakfast session on the radio. The presenters interlard their talk about traffic and weather with the odd witticism, and some of the songs they play have clever lyrics.

They read the paper. Debbie concentrates on the serious stuff on the first few pages, but Mark starts half-way through and finds lots of smart captions with alliteration, puns, and allusions. There's a report about a trial entitled *Prisoner free. Jury hung*, and an article by Germaine Greer in which she claims James Dean was gay. It is called *Mad about the Boy*, using the title of an old Noel Coward song. Some of the ads are witty too. One for lingerie catches Mark's eye, in which a scantily clad model says *Lola's Lingerie. I wear nothing else.*

They drive to work. A car in front of them has a bumper sticker that says *If you can read this, you're too close,* and Mark gets a black look from Debbie after being caught 'perving' on a blonde in a red sports car with the number plate *TOSEXI* (real example!).

On reaching the office Mark exchanges pleasantries with Declan, the security guard on the front desk, and Debbie engages in some banter with her aide, Cheryl. Mark opens his e-mail and among the Viagra ads he finds that someone has sent him a joke about yesterday's news. Debbie finds that someone has sent her a page of humorous headlines including *Sex more common than thought.* Today she has to give an address to the branch managers who are in town for a refresher. She already has a few jokes to put into the first part of her talk, but she spots something else in the 'headlines' and adds that. A few minutes later she receives a text message on her mobile. Like all text messages, it makes clever use of abbreviations: *I C U WANT 2 B 1 2* 'I see you want to be one too'.

During a coffee break Mark's colleague, Paul, drops by to discuss sales figures, but not before telling Mark a smutty joke about

Michael Jackson. At lunch Mark and Debbie meet a few workmates and recount humorous experiences and the like. Before going back to work Mark has to pick out a birthday card for his father. There are quite a few funny ones to pick from. On the way back he witnesses a demonstration. The tertiary teachers are marching to protest against reductions in funding for universities and some of them are carrying placards with catchy slogans such as *No more cuts. We slave our butts*.

It is Friday, the end of the working week, so when the office closes, Mark and Debbie go off to a nearby pub with workmates for a drink. A lot of the conversation involves puns and smart remarks about their boss, who is said to be so thick-witted *that he would be out of his depth in a puddle*. At some point someone tells a joke, and that leads others to join in and tell more.

When Debbie and Mark get home and have dinner, they turn on the television and watch a couple of sitcoms, a comedy movie, and finally a stand-up comedian. Over the course of the evening they indulge in a bit of light-hearted banter. Mark boasts about his prowess in the bedroom and Debbie puts him down.

Language lends itself to humour. It evolves. It is not designed by committee. This means that it is full of all kinds of ambiguities. Some words sound the same as others, which allows for puns: *I'm a baker because I knead the dough*. Some sequences admit of more than one interpretation as with *Killer sentenced to die twice* or *I saw a man eating a pizza and a dog* (perhaps it was a hot dog!).

Exploiting the humorous possibilities in language obviously provides entertainment, but people also use verbal humour for other ends: to establish harmony or rapport, to ingratiate themselves, to lighten the mood when contentious issues are raised, and to soften the force of criticism. There is a growing body of evidence that humour makes for better health and helps relieve stress, and some companies employ humour consultants in the hope of improved communication and productivity, and employee motivation.

While humour can build rapport in the short term, it can unite groups of people in the long term because it exploits local culture and local language, whether it be a matter of dialect or just local colloquialisms. The creating of an in-group sounds positive, but the creation of an in-group implies the creation of an out-group, and there's no doubt that humour has played a part in exclusion. There is thus a negative side to humour. It can be used to deride, to mock, to belittle, to stereotype. Too often in the past mainstream males have been the originators of humour, while women, ethnic minorities and people with disabilities have been the butt. But where people feel oppressed, they bond by sharing jokes at the expense of their oppressors, whether that be the enemy in war, slavers, prison guards, police, employers, the government, the ruling classes or, in the case of children, their teachers.

Joking is not entirely a light-hearted activity. If you stand back and look at the subject matter, you find that a lot of jokes deal with bodily functions or unpleasant human experiences such as death, disease, dismemberment and disfiguration, with the things we fear. Joking about these things seems to be a way of coping with unpleasant facts about our mortality. A lot of humour deals with war and poverty, indeed it has been said that humour is born of adversity. We are regularly counselled to talk about what troubles us. Joking seems to be a way of talking about our fears.

Comedy can also laugh us out of our follies. Comedians are social commentators. They are good at disturbing complacency, deflating egos, and exposing hypocrisy. They usually present an antidote to government propaganda. When the generals take over, comedians are suppressed. They must be doing something right.

There is a vast literature on jokes and at least one book just on laughter, but these writings are mostly about the psychology or sociology of humour. This book is mainly about the way we manipulate sounds, syllables, affixes, words, phrases, and constructions. It is full of funny examples. It is meant to be both instructive and enjoyable. As the old music hall master of ceremonies would have said, 'For your enjoyment and edification'. Read! Enjoy!

Lots of people have contributed to this book, most of them unwittingly. Kate Burridge pointed my way towards some nice sources of examples and made several helpful suggestions for improving the book, and Gavan Breen provided me with copious lists of howlers and the like. I only hope he does not find any more lurking in my text.

Barry Blake
Melbourne 2006

1

The nature of humour

One dictionary I consulted defined *humour* as 'the quality of being funny' and when I looked up *funny* it defined it as 'humorous'. To be fair, it also gave 'causing laughter' as one of the meanings of *funny*. I didn't feel like looking up *laughter* since we all know what laughter is. If you don't know what laughter is, you won't be able to find out from a dictionary definition. This reminds me of the story of the woman who once asked Fats Waller, 'Mr Waller. What is rhythm?' He replied, 'Lady, if you has to ask, I can't tell you.'

Whatever the dictionary says, laughter cannot be used as a touchstone for humour or funniness. Indeed, humour and laughter do not match. Let us consider a few examples.

Sometimes people laugh without there being anything funny. Most of us smile to show that we are friendly, for instance, in greeting friends or in over-the-counter dealings, but some people give a little laugh here and there, which is quite a useful device to keep things friendly, especially when the person you are talking to is out of sight. Recently a woman rang up a talk-back radio programme to seek advice about her dog from a guest vet. The vet asked what kind of dog she had and she replied that it was a Bassenji–Red Heeler cross. The presenter said that that sounded exotic, and the woman laughed. This laugh served to show she was accepting the comment in a good-natured way and that she recognized that this particular cross-breed was unusual.

To take another example. I was driving through a country town recently with my wife when I noticed that the van in front of us carried a sign *Barry Blake Outback Tours*. I burst out laughing at the coincidence between the tour operator's name and my own, but I wouldn't want to claim that this was humorous. It was more funny-peculiar than funny-haha.

Another example. While staying in Oxford a few years ago, my wife and I were invited to Jesus (College) for dinner. We found the right street with the help of a map, but we were uncertain exactly where the entrance to the college was. While we were looking lost, a young woman asked if she could help. I replied, 'We are looking for Jesus.' As soon as I said it, I couldn't help grinning, and the woman smiled too. In any other context this sentence would have had quite a different meaning. This is an example of unplanned, spontaneous humour. The double meaning arose unexpectedly, and the element of surprise, the sudden revelation of an alternative interpretation, is characteristic of humour.

Now for an example that is meant to be humorous, meant to be funny, meant to elicit laughter.

What do you get if you cross a computer with an icy road?
A hard drive.

Of course, I can't be certain that this is funny. In fact, I can be certain that some people, somewhere, will not find it funny. But it is in a joke format. If someone comes up to you and asks, 'What do you get if you cross a computer with an icy road?' and this question is irrelevant to the situation, you know that you have been given the feed line of a joke.

Now here's another example in the same format, but here I would judge that the joke is so weak that it is more likely to elicit a groan, a moue of disapproval or a real screwed-up face, the sort a child comes up with after taking nasty medicine.

What is the capital of England?
E.

These examples show that you can have laughter without humour and humour without laughter. Humour isn't always funny, but it is meant to elicit laughter or at least a smile, a grin, or some relaxation of the muscles around the mouth. Humour is universal, though what strikes some people as funny will not strike others in the same way. Humour can be in language or in action. If you want to get a laugh from people of virtually any culture, show someone all togged out in a fine white costume and then have them slip and fall in the mud. If you can establish that the person is an unsympathetic character, someone who is arrogant, for instance, all the better. In vaudeville and in silent movies and early talkies a common source of humour was throwing custard pies. It was thought to be very funny if someone threw a custard pie and hit someone else fair in the face. Better still if the victim ducked in anticipation and the pie hit an unsuspecting bystander. Laughing at someone's misfortune seems to be universal, and the bigger the accident the greater the potential for humour. Mel Brooks once said, 'Tragedy is if I cut my finger. Comedy is if I walk into an open sewer and die.'

Falling in the mud or into an open sewer is humour in action. In this book I will deal only with verbal humour, though a large proportion of jokes do deal with unfortunate accidents such as falling in the mud, or worse.

Principles of humour

There are no rules to be followed that will enable us to be funny or witty, but looking at examples reveals a number of recurrent properties. The overriding principle of humour is that there should be a **set-up** and a **punch**. We usually talk about a 'punchline', but the bit that makes the impact is not always a line. Some jokes take the form of short anecdotes, often with three episodes. The first two episodes form the set-up and the last the punch or punchline. Other jokes have a feed line and a punchline. Consider the following:

My husband and I divorced because of religious differences.
He thought he was God and I didn't.

The first sentence is the feed line and the key phrase is 'religious differences'. This leads you to expect that one partner in the marriage was Protestant and the other Catholic, or that one was Jewish and the other Christian, and then this expectation is shattered in the punchline, where 'religious differences' is given an unexpected interpretation. As in boxing, a good punch should not be telegraphed. It should come as a surprise, a sudden flash, a sudden revelation that there was another possible interpretation. In some instances the **set-up** and **punch** occur within a single statement. Consider the following 'headline'.

Injured upholstery worker fully recovered

You can easily read this and take it seriously, and if it were accompanied by an article detailing the convalescence of an injured worker, you might go on blissfully unaware that there was a humorous reading. If you are alert, and certainly if you find this example in a list of humorous headlines, you suddenly see that *upholstery* sets up the pun in *recovered*. The same situation is found in the next example,

Monogamy leaves a lot to be desired.

You first read the well-known idiom *leaves a lot to be desired* and give it the normal interpretation of 'being deficient'. Then you realize, in the context of *monogamy*, it is possible to take *desired* in one of the other senses that it has outside the idiom. There is a variant of this joke: *Celibacy leaves a lot to be desired*. The difference between monogamy and celibacy is small but significant.

This book is concerned with verbal humour, but some verbal humour revolves around incongruities of situation and the like, and does not depend on properties of language. Consider the following report from a local newspaper.

Two horse blankets were stolen from a stable near the racecourse last night. The horses noticed their blankets were missing around 11.30.

It is not certain whether this is serious reporting or an attempt at humour. There is certainly something funny about the notion of horses being the ones to notice their blankets were missing, but the humour does not arise from properties of language.

Fun with words

Each language contains thousands of words. They are stored in the brain in a kind of mental dictionary or lexicon. Since languages evolve and are not made up by a committee (Thank God!), it can happen that two or more words come to be pronounced alike, such as *peace* and *piece*. This is **homophony**. Moreover, many words have more than one meaning. Consider, for instance, some of the words for parts of the body that have extended meanings. We can talk of the *head of the school*, *the back of the bus*, *the mouth of the river* and *the foot of the hill*. This is **polysemy**. Homophony and polysemy allow us to make puns. Of the jokes and other witticisms that depend on language, probably a majority involve a pun.

When the actress saw her first grey hairs, she thought she'd dye.

How did the cat stop the VCR?
It pressed the paws button.

Dryden called the pun 'the lowest and most grovelling kind of wit'. But while it is true that puns are easy to make and can be so excruciatingly contrived as to elicit a groan rather than a laugh, they remain very popular. Puns not only appear in the punchline of a joke, as in the *die/dye* example above, they can also be slipped into conversation or into a piece of writing without disturbing the flow. They are also common in book titles, headlines and captions in newspapers and magazines (other than those reporting disasters), in greeting cards, and in advertising. Puns can be based on phrases as well as on single words. Here are some phrasal puns.

Why did the bank robber saw the legs off his bed?
Because he wanted to lie low for a while.

I'm very annoyed with my masseur.
He rubs me the wrong way.

There is also humour to be found in the mispronunciation, misidentification, and misuse of words. Most of this arises by accident, but the possibility can be exploited. Some mispronunciations are funny, particularly if they happen to result in a rude word. For instance, a recent TV news report was read as follows: 'British police are refusing to confirm media reports that a man was killed in last night's bum boss—bus bomb—in London.' Similarly, the wrong word in a particular context can be funny. Examples of this are not normally one-off slips, but the result of long-term ignorance, as when people say *mitigate against* for 'militate against'. I remember once catching an international beauty contest on TV (quite by accident, you understand) where the finalists were expected to say one sentence about their home country. The US entrant said that 'America was the land of *opportunism*.'

Another kind of error involves putting the wrong interpretation on what is heard. There is a well-known story of a young child who had a teddy bear whose eyes were askew, to which he gave the unusual name of *Gladly*. When he (the child, not the bear) was questioned about his choice of name, he said, 'It was from that song we sing in church, *Gladly the cross-eyed bear* ("Gladly the cross I bear").'

Grammatical ambiguities

When we hear someone speak or when we read a text, we have to identify the words (Is it *butt* 'stump' or *butt* 'barrel'?) and construe the sequence of words, that is, we must work out how they fit together. Consider the following example.

A: It's hard to get boys to wash.
B: Oh, I don't know. There are lots of dirty boys around.

A's statement is ambiguous. The most likely interpretation in our culture is that boys are not too keen on washing themselves, but as you can see from B's reply, there is another way of interpreting the sequence, namely, that it is hard to find boys that one could wash.

In the next example we have two sentences that look to be structurally similar since they differ only in the choice of the final noun.

I feel like a drink.
I feel like a fool.

However, they are understood in quite different ways. The first could be paraphrased as 'I feel that I would like to have a drink' and the second as 'I feel that I am like a fool'. This structural ambiguity is exploited in a number of jokes along the lines of the following.

The old master: I really am in good form this morning. I feel like a twenty-year-old.
Manservant: I'll have one sent up right away, m'lord.

Now consider the sentence *My mother made me a pullover*, which could be paraphrased as 'My mother made a pullover for me'. Next consider the sentence *My mother made me a laughing-stock* [which she might do if the pullover were like those featured in the Bridget Jones movies!]. This sentence has the same sequence of nouns and verbs and what have you, but it is interpreted quite differently. It could be paraphrased 'My mother made me to be a laughing-stock'. Now here is a joke exploiting the ambiguity of such sequences. I first saw it as a piece of graffiti, and it goes like this:

My mother made me a homosexual.

And added underneath:

If I sent her the wool, would she make me one too?

The joke lies on a certain background assumption, as indeed most jokes do. There is a theory bandied about to the effect that mothers can influence their sons to be homosexual by treating them too softly, by mollycoddling them. This background leads to a certain interpretation of the feed line, which is then shattered by the follow-up, which puts an unlikely interpretation on the feed line. Note that I am using the term 'feed line' even though the first line purports to be an independent statement and the punchline to be an independent comment. But though this is presented as a graffiti joke where one person comments on the work of another, it is quite likely that the same person wrote both lines. After all, who would bother to inscribe just the first line?

Transpositions

A lot of witticisms involve swapping words or parts of words around. The starting-point is usually a well-known expression. The following example is from Mae West, the buxom blonde star of Hollywood movies in the 1930s, whose amplitude was commemorated by her name being given to inflatable life jackets. This example is a transposition of the type known as **chiasmus** after the Greek letter *chi* (shaped like the letter X). I've written the second part of the quotation beneath the first and drawn in the chiasmus.

It's not the men in your life that counts.

It's the life in your men.

Some transpositions merely involve the switching of sounds between two words. These are called spoonerisms (see Chapter 10).

A behaviourist is someone who pulls habits out of rats.

This is an ingenious example is that it plays on 'pulling rabbits out of hats', which magicians do, and produces something that makes perfect sense.

Mixing styles

We don't all speak the same way, and no one speaks the same way all the time. In many societies, including our own, there are differences of language correlating roughly with where you stand on the socio-economic scale, and in almost all languages there are also differences of language dependent on where you come from. More importantly, there are differences of style, and most people command a repertoire of styles, including a formal style for conducting serious business and an informal style for use among friends and family. All these forms of variation can be exploited for humorous purposes. For instance, there is humour to be found in mixing styles or using an inappropriate style.

There is a very good example of the humorous effect of using a particular variety of language in the wrong context in Shaw's *Pygmalion*, better known to the present generation through the musical version *My Fair Lady*. When the Cockney flower girl, Eliza Doolittle, has been taught by Professor Henry Higgins to talk posh, that is, to use Received Pronunciation (BBC English), she is taken to tea with his mother, where she ventures to try out her new accent. Unfortunately, she has not been taught the socially acceptable forms of grammar to go with the new speech, so she says things such as, 'Somebody pinched it; and what I say is, them as pinched it done her in.' This kind of thing elicits laughter from Freddy Eynsford Hill and Eliza asks him, 'If I was doing it proper, what was you laughing at?' Certainly the incongruity of the posh accent and the Cockney grammar is funny, and it is designed to get laughs from the audience as well as from Freddy.

One form of humour used by amateur wits and professional comedians alike is to mock pomposity or pretension. One way they do this is to appear to misunderstand a word or phrase that they judge to be over-learned. A typical example can be found in the following exchange between two sports commentators talking about a star football recruit.

> **A: He's certainly very good. Where does he come from?**
> **B: He's domiciled in Newcastle.**
> **A: Yeah, but where does he live?**

A variation on a standard joke about pricking pretension goes like this.

> **A: My father is the conductor of the London Symphony Orchestra.**
> **B: My father is a conductor too.**
> **A: Oh, where does he do his conducting?**
> **B: On the Hammersmith bus.**

This is an example of **bathos**, the sudden switch from the serious to the ridiculous, from the high-falutin to the low. A more sophisticated example of bathos is found in the following passage from Woody Allen.

> **He was writing an Ethics, based on the theory that 'good and just behavior is not only more moral but could be done by phone.' Also, he was halfway through a new study of semantics, proving (as he so violently insisted) that sentence structure is innate but that whining is acquired.**

Americans have a character called Schwartz who is a stock figure of jokes like the 'conductor' one. Schwartz is the plain, ordinary man. Some years ago Cyd Charisse, the famous dancing star
of 1950s MGM musicals, was appearing in a stage production.
One of the celebrities interviewed outside the theatre on the opening night said he was looking forward to seeing the show, particularly as he knew Cyd. 'Oh,' said the interviewer, sounding
surprised, 'You know Cyd Charisse?' 'No,' replied the celebrity.
'Sid Schwartz. He plays third ukulele in the band.'

There are a number of humorous remarks attributed to Sam
Goldwyn (the 'G' of MGM). In the following example he appears
to misunderstand a not-too-learned word.

**Producer: I'm not sure about the script of this comedy.
It's too caustic.**

**Goldwyn: The hell with the cost. If it's good, we'll go
ahead.**

Another variation on the learned-versus-simple theme involves
an unsophisticated person failing to understand a 'hard word'.
There is a film called *Wit*, in which Emma Thompson plays a
professor of English who is diagnosed with ovarian cancer. Most
of the film shows Emma Thompson undergoing a long course of
extremely unpleasant chemotherapy, with hair loss and nausea.
The treatment fails and the cancer spreads. Emma is terminal.
Now there is nothing left but to administer drugs to relieve the
pain. Emma asks the nurse who is filling a hypodermic, 'Is what
you are giving me soporific?' The nurse replies, 'I don't know
about that, but it will sure put you to sleep.' Emma bursts out
laughing. The nurse asks why. Emma explains, and the nurse laughs
too. *Wit* is a harrowing film about an unpleasant subject. The
long story of the debilitating and degrading illness is part of the
set-up. There is also a more specific set-up in that the word *soporific* is illustrated earlier in the film. The joke is particularly funny
in context, since it relieves the horror of what is happening to the
patient.

Official language can often be pompous, stilted and obscure, and it invites derision. I never cease to wonder when I'm instructed to 'deplane the aircraft' why I couldn't be told it's all right to get off the plane. Not long ago it was not uncommon to see signs at railway stations *Do not expectorate*. This isn't very helpful when one considers that the sort of person likely to spit in public is hardly likely to know what this unusual learned word means. I remember seeing such a sign where someone had added underneath *Is it OK to spit?*

Language in context

As can be seen from the preceding sections, word forms can be ambiguous and so can sequences of words. But puns and structural ambiguity apart, there can still be more than one interpretation of a sentence. Language would be tedious if we specified what we mean in great detail. The way language works is that the speaker or writer gives enough detail for the addressee to be able to interpret the sentence in context. The following example would make sense in its original context, namely, the heading of a report on a committee decision to try and re-employ members of the oldest profession in one or other profession of shorter ancestry.

Committee wants prostitutes to be taught new skills.

However, since the new skills are not specified, the sentence could be about a plan to increase the professional repertoire of the women in question, an unlikely interpretation but a humorous possibility.

Lack of specification is particularly noticeable in the abbreviated text of recipes, notices and classified ads and on bottles of medicine, where one can find directions such as *Take one pill after each meal. Keep away from children.*

Dashing expectations

Most jokes lead the audience in one direction and set up the expectation of a certain outcome, only to introduce the unexpected in the punchline. Of course, this is true of many jokes involving puns and ambiguous sequences, but one can have humour just on the basis of the unexpected. Suppose you ask someone if they can write shorthand and they answer 'yes', you would understand them to mean that they were accomplished enough to get the benefit of the time-saving that shorthand offers. But suppose they answer, 'Yes, but it takes longer.' The expectation raised by 'yes' is immediately shattered. Jokes of this type do not depend on homophony, polysemy, or structural ambiguity. They can usually be translated from one language to another.

In the first example below we start with the first line of a rhyming couplet that is common in jokes. We expect a rhyme, in fact we expect 'you', but we don't get it.

Roses are red, violets are blue, I'm schizophrenic, and so am I.

The next examples involve the joker exploiting the fact that the first statement raises the expectation of a large number.

The Prime Minister was sixty yesterday and his wife put on a party and invited all his friends, but neither could come.

The President will leave today for a tour of friendly countries. He is expected back tomorrow.

The examples above are deliberate attempts at humour, but the following is an apparently serious report from a newspaper,

Mr Kanso Yoshida, cousin of Emperor Hirohito of Japan, has died in Liverpool aged 78. Since he came to Liverpool in 1912, Mr Yoshida has been known as Paddy Murphy.

Clever connections

A lot of creative work involves seeing a new analogy, that is, seeing a similarity or parallel between two situations, incidents, statements, people or whatever. As I write this I see a newspaper on the table with a cartoon by Wiley under the *Non Sequitur* rubric. It shows a caveman drawing a bison on the wall of a cave. Behind him is seated a cave boy (or perhaps a cave girl—it's hard to tell with cave kids). The cave boy throws a pebble and hits the man (his father?) on the back of the head and he says, 'Now draw a horse.' The caption reads *The first remote*. Wiley has picked out a clever analogy between the cave scene and modern TV with its remote control.

Some humour is of this type, deriving from the author seeing a connection between two seemingly disparate phenomena or entities. Language plays some part, but the primary source of humour lies in the relationship between the items referred to, which comes out in the punchline. Let's try an example.

Gracie Mitchell, who had been a stripper in her youth, was now in an old people's home. One day she got on the gin and in a fit of devilment decided to streak around the premises in the raw. As she flashed by, one elderly woman said to another, 'What was that lady wearing?' The other replied, 'I don't know, but it needs ironing.'

This picks out the resemblance between the seersucker appearance of old flesh and the crinkly appearance of unironed cloth.

Logic, or lack thereof

Unclear thinking can provide some funny moments. Sometimes it's a matter of circularity, other times an oxymoron or just vacuity.

Sports broadcasters often come out with a **tautology**, a kind of vacuity in which an unnecessary word or words are added that simply repeat the sense already given. A few such expressions are sanctioned by custom such as the phrase 'for sure and certain', but nonce examples simply reflect lapses of concentration or long-term ignorance. One sports commentator spoke of 'perfection at its best', another said, 'There wasn't anything of that sort of ilk', and a third said, 'It's not sufficient enough'. In these examples there is obviously a redundant word, but what about the radio personality who talked about a *false wig*. It sounds all right until you try to imagine what a 'true wig' might be. Much the same applies to the institution that employs *guidance counsellors*. Surely if they are counsellors they offer counsel or guidance. A recent dictionary defines 'prairie oysters' as 'discarded testicles from a male calf'.

Public figures, whether in sport, show business or politics, often make vacuous statements. Discussion about the future brings out the worst. One sports commentator offered his audience *a preview of the future*, and a politician told us solemnly that *the future is still to come*. Some of their other lapses in logic can be amusing. One sports commentator remarked that *He had seen cricket all over the world, and in other countries too* and another said *The statues will stand there in perpetuity for one year exactly*. One politician said *We were all unanimous*. Sounds sensible until you think about it. He could hardly have said *Some of us are unanimous*.

The following examples are jokes, though anyone familiar with the logic of sports commentators, television personalities and politicians might wonder if they are not records of real confusion.

Pizza man: Would you like this pizza cut into six pieces or eight?
Customer: Six, please. I couldn't eat eight.

Suicidal twin kills sister by mistake!

A man who learns that his nephew is entering the church says, 'I hope to live to hear you preach my funeral homily.'

Lawyer: This condition you've described, does it affect your memory at all?

Witness: Yes.

Lawyer: And in what ways does it affect your memory?

Witness: I forget things.

Lawyer: You forget. Can you give us an example of something that you've forgotten?

Satire, parody, irony, and sarcasm

In *Hamlet* Polonius tells Laertes that 'brevity is the soul of wit' and this book confines itself to brief humour, to examples that take no more than a few lines. Some forms of humour are usually long, consisting of a short story or even a whole novel. The most common of these is satire. **Satire** aims to ridicule, to prick pretensions, to expose hypocrisy, to show that appearances can often be deceptive. Satire distorts and exaggerates. The targets for satire are often governments, politicians, the military or the church, the upper or middle classes, the class system or the conventions of social life. The novels of Jane Austen, Dickens, Orwell, Huxley and, more recently, Heller and Roth are largely satirical. Most of Evelyn Waugh's novels are humorously satirical, including *Decline and Fall* and *Vile Bodies*, as are the libretti of W. S. Gilbert. Satire is necessarily humorous. Some of the humour is likely to be found in perceived incongruities of behaviour, for instance, the discrepancy between a politician's pronouncements on family values and his personal perversions. But there can also be verbal satire. Oscar Wilde's plays are lightly satiric. The satire comes through not only in the plot but also in witty repartee and what are now called 'one-liners' (examples are given in Chapter 8).

One device of satire is the grouping of the incongruous. In Waugh's *Black Mischief*, the Emperor of Azania, a mythical African state, begins his letter to King George V of England thus: *From Seth, Emperor of Azania, Chief of Chiefs of Sakuyu, Lord of Wanda and Tyrant of the Seas, Bachelor of Arts of Oxford University, to His Majesty of the King of England, Greeting.* Most of the grand self-description is what we might expect of a potentate, but the inclusion of BA (Oxon) is incongruous, and makes us wonder about Seth's perspective.

Another characteristic of satire is exaggeration. The next example is from Jay Leno, host of NBC's *The Tonight Show*. It went on air not long after the USA invaded and took control of Iraq. It too involves some exaggeration about the extent of corruption in America. Presumably there's enough for the audience to relate to.

Now there are reports from Baghdad that officials are taking bribes for favors, giving jobs to their relatives, taking money under the table from contractors. You know what this means? The war is less than a week old, and already they have an American-style democracy.

One form of satire is **parody**. One can parody any form of artistic expression, whether it be literary such a poem, a story, a religious text, a non-fictional text, a novel, a film or a play, or other forms such as paintings, ballet, music, especially opera and songs generally. The parody must be parallel with the original and the audience must be able to match the distortions and incongruities of the parody point by point with the original. Often this parallel extends over a long passage or even a whole work, and lies outside the scope of this book, but there can be local, small-scale parodies as part of a larger satire. In *The Loved One* Waugh satirizes the attention rich Americans lavish on their pets, focusing on a pet cemetery where all the rituals associated with human death are performed for animal deaths. At the funeral of a canine pet the following prayer is offered, a parody of what is recited at a human church service, 'Dog that is born of bitch hath but a short time to live, and is full of misery.'

Besides parodies of particular works there can be parodies of a certain genre. Here is a parody of the overblown style of the voice-over in a television documentary on the life of someone famous:

> **Looking at this humble cottage behind me it is hard to believe that we are standing in front of the birthplace of a man who would change forever the way we live. After him life would never be the same again.**
>
> **Raymond Baker left school at the age of 15 and took a job in a sawmill, and it was there that he conceived of the idea of sliced bread, when, eating his lunch at his workbench, he dropped his roll into the path of a circular saw. Now it is hard to believe today that up to the middle of the last century people bought bread in one solid mass and had to cut it themselves with a breadknife, a process which invariably resulted in a pile of crumbs and, if the operator wasn't careful, occasionally a splatter of blood or occasionally a small piece of finger.**

Parodies of songs and poems can be short. Some examples of parodies of rhymes are given in Chapter 11.

In the history of literature the term **burlesque** rivals parody and the two terms were to a great extent interchangeable, though burlesque perhaps tended to be used of mockery of a genre rather than of a particular work and was especially applied to theatrical parody. In the nineteenth century, in the USA, burlesque performances were ribald and featured scantily clad women. Eventually the term came to signify a lowbrow type of theatre with striptease the main attraction. This type of show lasted until the middle of the twentieth century. Exhibits at the Exotic World Burlesque Museum in Helendale, California, include pasties, garter belts, and G-strings. That gives a pretty good idea of what burlesque came to mean.

Irony is used in a number of senses. Some would call it ironical if the man who invented the guillotine was the first person to be executed by it, but the more central meaning of irony involves a character being unaware of something that is obvious to another character in a story and/or the author and audience. The story of King Oedipus provides a classic example. Oedipus hears a prophecy that he is destined to kill his father and marry his mother, so he leaves the ones he believes to be his parents and goes to another kingdom. However, he does not know that he has been reared apart from his real parents and thus, in an attempt to avoid his fate, enters his father's kingdom and fulfils the prophecy. This is sometimes called tragic irony.

An example of humorous, verbal irony is provided by the following anecdote, which, I am assured, is authentic. Certainly I have encountered other instances of the same kind of thing. A man was criticized for his accent, someone chiding him for pronouncing *fine* as 'foine'. He replied indignantly, 'Oi never say *foine*.' But he repeated the alleged error in his pronunciation of 'I', since presumably this was his regular pronunciation of the diphthong that occurs in 'I', 'fine', etc., his reply giving the lie to his protestation of innocence.

In a standard example of this kind of irony someone unwittingly reveals the very fault they are accused of. A woman accused of being pretentious replies indignantly, 'Pretentious? Moi?' There is the story of a man acquitted of robbing a bank. When the judge announced that he was free to go, he asked, 'Does this mean I can keep the money?' And there are also reports, of dubious authenticity, of ads in the newspaper directed to the blind and commercials on the radio directed to the deaf.

When I was about nine years old, a girl who lived across the road came over and gave me her Bible, the Authorized Version, telling me that since she was graduating from Sunday school, she wouldn't be needing it again. I'm sure she didn't mean that she was upgrading to the Revised Version.

The following example is from Samuel Butler's *Note-Books*.

A little boy and a little girl are looking at a picture of Adam and Eve.

'Which is Adam, and which is Eve?' said one.

'I don't know,' said the other, 'but I could tell if they had their clothes on.'

To me this is the essence of irony, the incongruity between the innocence or ignorance of a participant and the knowledge of the author and audience.

There is an old joke about a psychologist who is invited to give a lecture on sex. Too embarrassed to tell his wife that he has been hired to talk on this unmentionable subject, he tells her that he is going to talk about horse-riding. A few days later a woman who has attended the talk runs into the wife and tells her how much she enjoyed it. The wife replies, 'I'm surprised. The first time he tried it he fell off, and the next time he lost his whip.' Neither woman has the complete picture; only the reader is in a position to appreciate the irony.

There is a kind of irony too in a statement like the following, attributed to the Irish politician Sir Boyle Roche (1743–1807), where the force of what he has said appears to have been lost on the speaker. It is quoted in Shipley as an example of the kind of nonsense known as an Irish Bull.

Half the lies our opponents tell about us are not true.

The next example is a story joke in the common three-episode form. The irony of the interviewee's last statement is obvious, and reflects a bitter truth about the 'Troubles' in Northern Ireland.

When the Troubles in Northern Ireland were at their height an American radio journalist was sent to interview representatives from the Protestant and Catholic sides. Here is a transcript of his interview with Michael O'Leary.

Interviewer: Now, Mr O'Leary. Are you a Catholic?

O'Leary: When those Protestants march down the street, who do you tink it is who trows rocks roight trough the big bass drum?

Interviewer: Yes, but are you a Catholic?

O'Leary: When tose bombs go off in Protestant pubs, who do you tink plants 'em?

Interviewer: Yes, but I want to know if you are a Catholic. Do you go to Mass?

O'Leary: Aren't I after saying tat I'm a Cat'lic? But I'm not a fanatic.

Another example of ironic ignorance in the context of religious differences is to be found in the reporter who described a popular theatre as a 'Mecca' for Jewish theatre-goers. Some further examples of verbal irony are given under 'Oxymora' in Chapter 7.

Closely related to irony is sarcasm, sometimes described as 'the lowest form of wit', though the origin of this quote remains obscure. **Sarcasm** is more direct than irony and usually involves someone saying something that is the opposite of what is appropriate, often in a derisive or mocking tone. Some people extend the term 'irony' to cover what I am calling sarcasm, but that blurs an important distinction. For me irony essentially involves someone being blind to the significance of an event or a statement while another participant or just the author and audience are aware of the ignorance.

There are some well-established sarcastic formulas in the lexicon. For instance, if you have occasion to pay somebody a very small sum of money, the expression to use in this situation is 'Don't spend it all at once.' To somebody who seems to be in an unnecessary hurry, you say, 'Where's the fire?' Obviously, there's no fire. You are chiding the over-anxious person and trying to get them to relax and go about what they are doing more slowly. If a child returns unexpectedly quickly from an errand, you can say, 'What kept you?' In many situations there is no ready-made expression available, but one might feel sarcasm appropriate. For instance, a boy cuts his finger and makes a lot of fuss about it, so someone says, 'Do you want me to call an ambulance?'

Sometimes sarcasm misfires. Suppose a woman from a group of acquaintances gets up and sings 'Amazing Grace'. A member of the group, critical of the performance, remarks to another, 'What a fantastic singer she is!' The addressee might be uncertain about the quality of the singing and in doubt as to whether to take the statement at face value.

2
What do people joke about?

Some jokes require nothing more than that the joker and the audience share the same language. This is true of a lot of puns. But most jokes require a shared culture. In order to put a successful joke across, the joker needs to know whether the audience has the knowledge to get the joke and whether the audience thinks the subject is a suitable topic for humour.

The cultural background

If we were to go back to the seventeenth century, we could fairly easily describe the culture of pretty well all English speakers. Almost everyone would have been familiar with certain characters and episodes from the Bible, and educated people would have been familiar with classical works such as Homer's *Iliad* and Vergil's *Aeneid*. Cultural knowledge would not have changed much from generation to generation. Nowadays English is spoken by a great variety of people around the world with different cultures, and even within a particular nation such as the United Kingdom there are numerous aspects of culture that are not shared by the whole community. These include cricket, pop music, and computers. This means that a lot of jokes will not work across the whole community. Take references to computers, for instance. I read somewhere that Thomas Watson, the head of IBM, said many years

ago that there would be a world market for 'maybe five computers'. This seems universally funny now, because everybody knows
how computers have proliferated. However, when Bill Gates, the
head of Microsoft, is quoted as having said in 1981 that '640K
ought to be enough for anybody', this seems funny in light of the
enormous expansion of computer memory, but '640K' will mean
something only to those who know about computers. When you
visit granny in the nursing home, it's no good telling her computer jokes to cheer her up.

It is probably still true that the Bible is the most widely known
book, though nowadays knowledge of it is very much on the
wane. From the Old Testament people are generally familiar with
the stories of Adam and Eve, Noah's Ark, Moses, David and
Goliath, and Samson and Delilah, and there are jokes about all
these people. From the New Testament certain stories are particularly well known, such as the Prodigal Son, Jesus turning water
into wine, walking on water and raising Lazarus back to life. Again,
there are jokes based on these passages from the New Testament,
and it is regular for sports commentators to refer to teams getting
up to win from an impossible position as 'making the greatest
comeback since Lazarus'. Whether you are a Christian or not, you
have to know certain things in order to get a large class of jokes
about Hell (where bad people go when they die) and Heaven
(where good people go). Entrance to Heaven is via the Pearly
Gates and these are under the control of St Peter, who looks over
your record and decides where you finish up.

Some of the plays of Shakespeare are well known, particularly
Hamlet and *Romeo and Juliet*. Certain stories and characters from
history are also familiar. In the English-speaking world these include figures such as Julius Caesar, Anthony and Cleopatra (all
three with the help of Shakespeare), King Alfred (who burned
the cakes), Henry VIII (who had too many spouses) and Elizabeth I (who had too few), plus a set of characters from the Robin
Hood stories. For Americans you could add people such as George
Washington, who, among other things, cut down a cherry tree. It
is a feature of the present time that much this traditional knowledge is not widely known among young people.

Shared knowledge also includes political figures such as prime ministers and presidents, sports stars such as David Beckham, Michael Schumacher, and Venus and Serena Williams, pop music performers from Abba to Madonna, and film stars such as Julia Roberts, Tom Cruise and Arnold Schwarzenegger, plus certain films such as *Gone with the Wind*, *Casablanca*, *My Fair Lady*, and the *Star Wars* series.

It is not enough to know the names; often you need to know something about these people and films to get a particular joke. For instance, you need to know not only that Stevie Wonder is a pop star to get the following joke, but also that he is blind:

What did Stevie Wonder's partner do after they had had an argument?
Move the furniture around.

Obviously a good deal of shared knowledge is ephemeral. As the years go by certain figures fade into obscurity, to be replaced by others. In the 1930s one could joke that Mrs Simpson had *gone with the Windsor*, a reference both to the abdication of Edward VIII to marry her, and to the film *Gone with the Wind*. Some jokes can be recycled to apply to different people in different generations. Those that require a sex siren, for instance, or a dumb politician simply take a current example. There's no shortage.

The following is offered as an example of a joke that depends on a piece of ephemeral culture, but one of surprising longevity. The joke first, the discussion to follow.

A businessman takes his seat in a plane for a flight to Sydney and is delighted to find that a very attractive young woman is seated next to him. He strikes up a conversation.
'What are you off to Sydney for, if I may ask?' he enquires.
'I'm going to a conference on *Sex in the Twenty-first Century*,' she replies.

'Oh, are you giving a presentation?'
'I certainly am.'
'What is it about?'
'I'm going to expose a number of popular myths. It is commonly believed that Black men are the best endowed, but recent studies have shown that Native Americans are the best endowed. It is also commonly believed that the French and Italians are the most romantic lovers, but after an extensive investigation I have discovered that Jewish men are the best lovers.'
'That's very interesting,' says the businessman.
'By the way, I'm Gloria Stevenson,' says the young woman, 'and you are...?'
'Me? Oh, I'm Tonto, Tonto Silverstein.'

To get this joke you need to know that Silverstein is a Jewish name. That's not much of a problem. But you also need to know who Tonto is. In the 1930s there was a popular radio serial about a western hero called *The Lone Ranger*. He rode a white stallion (yes, stallion) called Silver to the strains of the William Tell overture, he wore a mask, and he had a catch-cry 'Hi-ho, Silver'. In those days heroes usually had a male companion and the Lone Ranger had a faithful Indian companion called Tonto (male companions were always faithful). There was also a television series that ran from 1949 till 1957, but the remarkable thing is that the Lone Ranger and Tonto figure in numerous jokes and allusions to this day. One standard reference is to be found in the 1998 film *Lolita*. The Jeremy Irons character is staying with a widow and her daughter, Lolita. One evening, the widow, who has her eye on Jeremy, tries get rid of young Lolita by saying, 'Isn't it time we were in bed?' Lolita replies, 'What's with the "we", paleface?' This is the punchline of a joke in which the Lone Ranger and Tonto find themselves surrounded by hostile Indians. The Lone Ranger says to Tonto, 'We are in big trouble, Tonto,' to which Tonto replies, 'What's with the "we", paleface?'

The Lone Ranger and Tonto jokes have had a great run, but unless there's a new television series, they are surely destined to fade from memory. While *The Lone Ranger* ran continuously for some years, the British television sit-com *Fawlty Towers* ran for only twelve episodes (six each in 1975 and 1979), yet it has put at least one phrase into general circulation, perhaps because the shows are frequently re-broadcast. In one episode German guests are expected at Fawlty Towers, a Torquay hotel, and the owner, Basil Fawlty (John Cleese), says to his staff, 'Don't mention the war.' Ironically, but predictably, Basil himself is the one to mention it. The phrase *Don't mention the war* is now in wide circulation, and people use it in a light-hearted way with reference to various subjects that they want kept quiet.

Trying to estimate whether your audience is familiar with *The Lone Ranger* or *Fawlty Towers* is a matter of hit and miss, but some esoteric knowledge is predictable for certain audiences. Where two people share a religion, a sport, an occupation or a hobby, they can share jokes relating to these interests that would be obscure to outsiders.

Beliefs and attitudes

Humour reveals a lot about people. Behind every joke there lurk shared folk beliefs and attitudes. Take the joke that says a camel is a horse designed by a committee. It involves an unfavourable view of camels and committees and a favourable view of horses.

A large proportion of jokes are racist in that they are based on the assumption that a certain race or nationality is lazy, dirty or stupid. Jokes in which a race or nationality is depicted as thick-witted are the most common, and much the same jokes are told by various peoples about other peoples they are in contact with. The English, for instance, tell Irish jokes, the Russians tell Ukrainian jokes, the Germans tell Polish jokes, the Dutch tell Flemish jokes, the Swedes tell Norwegian jokes, and the Canadians tell Newfie (Newfoundlander) jokes in both English and French. It cannot be assumed from a list like this that the Irish, Ukrainians and Poles, etc. do not tell racist-type jokes. The Irish, for instance, tell jokes about people from Cork and Kerry. In the ancient world the residents of certain cities were considered stupid and were the regular butt of jokes. These included Sidon (in present-day Lebanon) and Sybaris, a Greek city in southern Italy. Sybaris was famous for its wealth and easy living, hence the adjective *sybaritic*, so perhaps jealousy played some part in its being considered dumb. In many parts of the world city-dwellers tell jokes about rural people. This kind of attitude is common. In English the view that city people are sophisticated and country people unsophisticated is reflected in the language itself. Compare the positive words *urbane* (from Latin *urbs* 'city'), *politic* (from Greek *polis* 'city') and *civil* (from Latin *civis* 'citizen') against negative words such as *rustic*, *boor*, *peasant* and *clodhopper*, which relate to the country.

In English-language jokes one is expected to recognize certain stereotypes such as the mean Scotsman, the dumb Irishman, the precise German, the boastful American, the underendowed East Asian man, and the overendowed Black man. The French, the Spanish and the Italians are often considered to be great lovers, and to put great stock in romance, whether licit or illicit. In Edmond Rostand's well-known play *Cyrano De Bergerac* (1897), Roxanne manages to get through the Spanish lines at the siege of Arras to visit her husband. When the French ask her how she managed to do this, she replies that she told the Spanish guards she was visiting her lover, because if she had said she was visiting her husband, they would not have let her through.

In British folklore the French are always naughty. Paris is where you go for a dirty weekend. It is where you'll be offered *French prints* (pornographic pictures) and if you don't use a *French letter* (condom), you are likely to get a dose of the *French disease* (venereal disease). This attitude is reflected in the following exchange from Wilde's *The Importance of Being Earnest*.

Jack: He seems to have expressed a desire to be buried in Paris.

The Reverend Chasuble: In Paris! I fear that hardly points to any very serious state of mind at the last.

Jokes about nationalities need not be offensive. They operate on the basis of stereotypes. One particular feature, not necessarily anything too negative, is thought to be predominant in the behaviour of a particular country and it is picked out as characterizing that country. Getting jokes about nationalities often involves recognizing what the folklore takes to be the stereotype. The following ingeniously covers five stereotypes.

What is the difference between Heaven and Hell?

In Heaven, the English are the policemen, the French are the chefs, the Germans the mechanics, the Italians are the lovers, and the Swiss organize everything. In Hell, the Germans are the policemen, the English are the chefs, the French the mechanics, the Swiss are the lovers, and the Italians organize everything.

Jokes directed against a religion, a race, a nationality or an ethnic minority are sometimes told by the people who appear to be the butt of the joke. In collections of Jewish jokes one often finds examples of self-disparagement, but the alleged characteristic is usually not something people are likely to be ashamed of. Here is an example based on the prominence of Jews in commerce, a common theme in Jewish humour.

Why did God make goyim [gentiles]?
Somebody has to buy retail.

Until recently most jokes were made by men, so it is no surprise to find that quite a few jokes are at the expense of women. In some jokes women are represented as stupid, though many such jokes are confined to 'blondes', where 'blonde' is to be understood not as any female with blonde hair, but as a *bimbo*. The word *bimbo* is interesting. It is Italian for '(male) baby' and came into English first as a word for an effeminate male, but it soon came to refer to a woman more valued for her appearance than for her mental capacities. In jokes, men are assumed to be permanently lecherous. Well, there probably won't be too much debate about that. Women, on the other hand, are assigned to two quite different categories. Married women are generally represented as being insufficiently interested in sex to satisfy their husbands' libido, whereas unmarried females are either virgins or nymphomaniacs. In typical cartoons of yesteryear the wife was depicted as an overweight, middle-aged woman in a dressing-gown, with her hair in curlers, waiting with a rolling-pin in her hand for her husband to come home from late-night drinking (or worse).

There is a story about a man who goes to the doctor and is told that he has a dangerous heart condition.

> 'You'll have to take it easy, if you want to live,' says the doctor.
> 'What about smoking?' asks the man.
> 'No smoking,' says the doctor.
> 'What about drinking?'
> 'No drinking,' says the doctor.
> 'What about … ?'
> 'Only once a fortnight,' says the doctor, 'and with your wife. You mustn't risk any excitement.'

This reflects a male attitude that sex with one's wife is not exciting, whereas sex with a new partner would be. The joke might be considered anti-wife, but it can be turned against husbands. However, whether directed against wives or husbands it depends on accepting that conjugal copulation is dull compared with adultery. This idea that marriage is unattractive and monotonous, something like life in a medium-security prison, lies behind numerous jokes. Toscanini once reprimanded an orchestra at a rehearsal for their lack-lustre performance by pointing out that the musical direction was *con amore*, but they were playing like married men. W. C. Fields was once asked if married people lived longer. He said, 'No, it just seems longer.'

But while married women might be depicted as lacking in libido, jokes recognize a large class of available women, who inhabit a Utopia where all women are beautiful, they never get pregnant, and they are never infected with sexually transmissible diseases. One such woman figures in the following.

A young woman went to her beauty salon and asked for the full treatment: hair, face, nails, Brazilian, fake tan, you name it.
'What's this in aid of?' asked one of the beauticians.
'I'm going away for the weekend with a man,' the young woman replied.
'Oh,' said the beautician. 'Is it anyone you know?'

A piece of background essential for understanding some of the jokes from the colonial era was the notion that many 'natives' were cannibals and were likely to eat white settlers. In cartoons the cannibals were depicted as cooking their victims in a very large iron pot. It is this background that provides the humorous interpretation of a sentence like *The missionaries gave the cannibals their first taste of Christianity*, and lies behind a class of cannibal jokes (illustrated in Chapter 7).

Subject matter

If we hunt through references to humour in European history, we find that practical jokes have always been popular, including such childish practices as turning on fountains and sprinklers when guests were passing by. Retelling of practical jokes was common in verbal and written humour. There is a good example in Chaucer's *Miller's Tale* and it is one typical of its time. Alison and Nicholas have just had a night of adulterous love, when another would-be lover, Absolon, comes to serenade Alison. She agrees to one kiss, but makes him close his eyes. She then whips off her knickers and presents her posterior at the window, which Absolon unwittingly kisses. Nicholas and Alison laugh at Absolon, who promptly plots his revenge. He goes off to the blacksmith and gets a red-hot poker. He returns and asks for another kiss. Nicholas thinks he will have more sport at Absolon's expense, so he flashes his fundament at the window and farts in Absalon's face, only to get the red-hot poker up his bum.

From classical times right down until recently the repertoire of professional jokers included mockery, mimicry and insults. People with a speech impediment or an unfamiliar accent were fair game, as were cripples or anyone with any deformity. Even those considered ugly would be mocked. Among the ancient Greeks redheads and bald people were included, as well as people who had suffered some social disgrace. There were joke books or collections of jokes in the ancient world, and one collection from the sixth century AD reveals a large proportion of jokes directed against intellectuals, including professors, doctors and lawyers, and at the other end of the scale, allegedly stupid people. Over the last few centuries targets have included the simple-minded fool, the provincial, the peasant, the drunk, the mentally deranged, the elderly, the mother-in-law, the nagging wife, the hen-pecked husband, the clergyman, the politician, the old maid, the foreigner and the effeminate male.

Jokes about allegedly stupid people are very common today. Some are directed against a race or nationality, and others are directed against individuals, mostly politicians. Gerald Ford, Ronald Reagan, George Bush and George W. Bush have been popular butts for dumb jokes over the last thirty years, which is a bit of a worry when you consider the power American presidents have. Here are two samples.

From time to time the computers at the Pearly Gates go down and during such periods anyone wanting to get into Heaven has to provide evidence of their identity. For instance, when Einstein died, St Peter asked him to write down a few of his famous equations, and when Picasso died, St Peter asked him to do sketch versions of some of his best-known works. When Ronald Reagan died, St Peter

asked him to identify himself, but Ronald said he didn't know how he could do that.

St Peter explained, 'Einstein wrote down some of his famous equations and Picasso sketched some of his most famous works. What could you do, Ronald, to show you are who you say you are?'

Reagan replied, 'Who are Einstein and Picasso?'

'Don't worry,' said St Peter. 'That's gotta be you, Ronald. Come right in.'

George W. Bush and Dick Cheyney go into a restaurant. The President scans the menu and then asks the waitress for a quickie. She is a bit taken aback. 'Mr President, I didn't expect that kind of behaviour from you. With your predecessor, perhaps.'

The Vice-President leans across and whispers to his chief, 'George, it's pronounced *keesh*.'

Innumerable jokes are about misfortunes such as death, disease and mutilation (especially castration) and disabilities such as lacking a limb or being deaf, blind or dumb. Just after Christmas 2004 a tsunami wiped out over 200,000 people in Asia. It was one of the greatest tragedies of all time, but within a day or so the jokes were circulating: *Santa didn't have time to visit Asia this year, so he just gave them a wave.* The same with Hurricane Katrina, which devastated New Orleans in August 2005: *The first bar to re-open on Bourbon and Water Street found it didn't take long for the regular customers to drift in.* With every new event, whether it be the Falklands War, the First Gulf War, the invasion of Iraq or the London bombings of July 2005, old jokes are modified to fit the situation. The magnitude of the impact of the terrorist destruction of the twin towers of the World Trade Center in New York on 11 September 2001 was evident from the fact that it remained a no-no for comedians for some time after the event. Terrorist humour in general, however, is common nowadays, with lots of jokes about people like arch-terrorist Osama bin Laden, who has even been given a mythical brother, Hadn bin Laid. With every new invention such as the pill or Viagra there are jokes. In fact, there are probably as many Viagra jokes as there are unsolicited ads for the product on the internet. Examples include *Use Viagra eye-drops to give you a hard look* and *Viagra stolen. Police seek hardened criminals*.

It is only since roughly the 1960s that objections have been raised to racist and sexist jokes. With this enlightenment come jokes sympathetic to the victims of racism. The next example assumes a background of rampant racism and laughs at it.

A couple of indigenous Australians are walking home in Darwin when an old white man, tanked to the eyeballs, runs off the road, sends them flying, and then crashes into a tree. One of the Aborigines is thrown through the air and lands 50 yards down the road and the other is thrown through the front window of a house. When the police arrive, the drunk asks them whether there will be any charges.

'Too bloody right,' say the cops. 'We'll charge the one down the road with leaving the scene of an accident and the one in the house there with breaking and entering.'

Similarly with sexism, whereas once women were commonly the butt of men's jokes, nowadays there are female comedians and jokes aplenty at the expense of men.

Why do men like smart women? Opposites attract.

Equestrian activity teaches young women to cope with large, dumb but friendly beings—the ideal training for marriage.

When God created man she was only experimenting.

In the next example, we think we are hearing a traditional sexist joke, but the reverse turns out to be the case.

Why do women find it so hard to park close to the kerb?
Because they are used to being told that this (holding up a
finger) is 10 inches.

Besides jokes designed to denigrate another race or nationality, there are also jokes meant to bring out supposed positive traits. For example, there is the definition of a Jewish dropout: *a boy who didn't finish his PhD*. Politicians are regular butts of jokes, and understandably so. In the nature of things politicians tend to be selective in their arguments and inconsistent. They are under pressure at one time to make promises, and at another to break them. And of course from time to time the odd politician is caught involved in corruption or a sex scandal. As *Mad* magazine's familiar cartoon wisecracker Alfred E. Neuman once said, 'Crime does not pay ... as well as politics.'

Governments are always in disfavour with a fairly large proportion of the electorate, and repressive regimes create situations where one of the few recourses open to people is to laugh at their misery.

In Nazi Germany there were numerous anti-government jokes, especially when the war started going badly. People made fun of Hitler, Goebbels and especially Goering, and about the discrepancy between what the propaganda suggested and the grim reality. For a start there was the spectacular discrepancy between the fair, tall, slim Aryan ideal and the dark hair of Hitler, the shortness of Goebbels and the obesity of Goering. But one had to be careful: a joke like the following could have landed the teller in a concentration camp.

A German boy is taught by his father to say the following
grace before meals, 'I give thanks to God and the Führer
for the food I am about to receive.'
'But,' enquires the child, 'what do I say if the Führer dies?"
'Then,' replies the father, 'all you have to say is "I give
thanks to God".'

There were numerous jokes about the authoritarian regimes that existed behind the Iron Curtain and the austerity of the Cold War years.

A man goes into a Russian butcher's shop. He asks for two lamb chops. No lamb. He asks for a beefsteak. No beef. He asks for a pork tenderloin. No pork. When he leaves, the butcher turns to his assistant and says, 'What a memory!'

During the Cold War a number of jokes critical of the USSR were in the form of questions to and answers from Radio Armenia or Radio Yerevan. Yerevan was the capital of Soviet Armenia and there is in fact a station called Radio Yerevan, but none of the jokes could possibly have been broadcast from that censored source. It was said it offered a prize for the best political joke: ten years in a labour camp.

Question: What is the most *permanent* feature of our socialist economy?
Radio Armenia: *Temporary* shortages.

Question: What will be the results of the next elections?
Radio Armenia: Nobody can tell. Yesterday somebody stole the results of the next elections from the office of the Central Committee of the USSR.

Up till the 1960s it was common for comedians to play the drunk. This allowed them to do funny body language, funny logic and funny phonetics. This has pretty much gone out of fashion, though drunks still figure in some story-type jokes. Drinking alcohol is a major social activity for a minority, and a minority activity for a majority. It is accompanied by various conventions that range from announcing toasts and clinking glasses to arrangements for who pays. Although not a particularly salient subject for jokes, drinking is the focus for a lot of light-hearted raillery. In the first (authentic) example 'he' sees 'her' open a bottle of port and pour a drink. He goes away and returns a little over an hour later and notices the bottle is half empty.

He (disingenuously): Did you spill the bottle?
She: No. They're not filling them the way they used to.

The next example is concocted from two authentic examples.

A: Would you like a drink?
B: No, I don't think so.
A: Sure?
B: Oh, all right. You talked me into it.
C: I'd like one too.
A: I didn't need to ask you. You get withdrawal symptoms if you haven't had one by three o'clock.

Excessive drinking was probably more common in the past than it is now after many campaigns to curb driving under the influence. It has been common to boast about one's capacity to drink and how one drank to excess, with expressions like, 'I was bloody legless'. There are tales of drink-related mishaps such as the story of the man who went home drunk and got up during the night and peed in the closet—the closet, not the water-closet.

Popular butts for humour include mothers-in-law and lawyers. Mother-in-law jokes have a natural basis. When you marry, you are expected to be loyal to your spouse, but this can conflict with your duty to your parents. The conflict is probably greater for wives, since women tend to be closer to their mothers, and therefore ill feeling about interference is greater with husbands. In such jokes a man's mother-in-law is either interfering or overstays her welcome or both. In fact, there's a witty way of describing the stamina of a runner or racehorse, 'He stays like a mother-in-law'. Anyway, here are two examples of the genre.

Wife: The family that prays together stays together.
Husband: Thank God your mother's an atheist.

Three men were discussing what they would do if the doctor told them they had only two weeks to live. The first said he'd try to have sex every day for the whole fortnight. The second was a gourmet, so he said he'd have as many of his favourite dishes as he could. The third said he'd take his mother-in-law on a holiday. The other two were amazed at his choice and asked him why. 'It would be the longest two weeks of my life,' he replied.

Mother-in-law jokes are in decline, however, perhaps because in these more affluent times married couples and in-laws don't so often share the same premises.

Lawyer jokes are so popular that you can buy whole books of them. This seems strange to me. Most people have very few dealings with lawyers beyond the odd bit of conveyancing or handling a will, and I've rarely heard the profession criticized, except perhaps for criminal lawyers defending underworld figures. Anyway, for whatever reason, lawyers figure prominently in jokes and are depicted as dishonest. Will Rogers is quoted as having said *Make crime pay. Become a lawyer*, and there's a line that goes *99% of lawyers give the rest a bad name*. The unpopularity of lawyers seems to be greatest in the USA, where litigation is more frequent.

The Pope died and found himself in the queue outside the Pearly Gates waiting to get his place in Heaven. The man in front of him was a lawyer, and when St Peter got his record up on his screen, he smiled and said, 'Well done. Take this smart card. It is the key to the penthouse suite at the Hilton where you'll be staying for eternity.' The lawyer thanked St Peter and went through the gates. St Peter then brought the Pope's record up, scrutinized it, and gave the Pope a large key. Well, it wasn't exactly one of the keys of the kingdom, for St Peter said, 'This will let you into the back room of Luigi's Pensione. That's where you'll be accommodated for eternity.' 'But,' said the Pope, 'I was the head of the largest Christian church. How come I get a room in a pensione when that lawyer who was here a minute ago got a penthouse suite?' 'It's like this,' said St Peter. 'Over the centuries we've had a number of popes. In fact about 80% of them have made it to Heaven. But he's our first lawyer.'

Religious jokes are also popular. There are two types of theme. One is differences in religious practices, either between Christians and Jews or between Catholics and Protestants. Examples of the latter genre can be traced right back to the Reformation. Interestingly, there are no jokes about the Orthodox churches, at least in English. Out of sight, out of mind. The other theme is the unexpected naughtiness of a rabbi or priest, or better still, a nun. The following one is about a rabbi and a priest.

A rabbi and a priest were travelling in the same compartment in a train and fell to discussing the demands of their respective callings.
'Rabbi,' said the priest, 'I understand that you cannot eat pork.'
'Yes, that's true,' said the rabbi.
'But haven't you ever wondered what it tastes like? Haven't you ever snuk a bit when no one was looking?'
'Well, to tell you the truth,' the rabbi replied, 'I did try it once.'
After a pause, the rabbi went on, 'Father, isn't it true that you are not allowed to have a woman?'
'That's right,' said the priest.
'But haven't you ever been a bit naughty and found yourself a woman?'
The priest blushed and replied rather sheepishly, 'Just between you and me, I have a parishioner who's rather free with her favours and I have made the odd pastoral call.'
'Better than pork, isn't it?' replied the rabbi.

The rabbi-and-priest joke also involves sex. Probably a majority of jokes, at least in Western society, deal with sex or other bodily functions. Freud wrote that, 'It is curious that common people so thoroughly enjoy such smutty talk, and that it is a constant feature of cheerful humour.' The common people are contrasted with the refined and cultured social stratum, where the smut must be witty. Within the sexual area, so to speak, there are jokes about infidelity, impotence, premature ejaculation, periods, unwanted pregnancy, sexually transmissible diseases and castration. Quite a few jokes are about the inexperience of honeymooners. These seem rather quaint now, since most couples put in a pretty solid pre-season before formalizing their union.

A popular genre of sexually oriented jokes deals with the doctor and patient, and, need I tell you, the doctor is a male and the patient a young attractive female. For instance, I remember seeing a cartoon showing a doctor coming from behind a screen and saying, 'All right, you can get dressed again, Miss Brown. It's just as I thought. You do have a sore throat.' When men consider the medical profession, one of the first advantages they think of is that it allows male doctors access to attractive, young, female bodies. There's a certain voyeuristic element in jokes of the doctor–female patient genre, as in the next example.

After an operation a young woman goes back to her doctor to have the stitches out. 'Will the scar show?' she asks. 'That's up to you,' replies the doctor.

Besides straight-out references to sex, there is also the use of words that are similar to terms connected with sex or other bodily functions. The straight man might say, 'He got into a lot of trouble. They castigated him.' The comedian will wince and hold his crotch, suggesting he has taken the learned word to refer to castration. Another variation goes like this. The comedian is reading a report about the royal family. He pauses and shows the report to his assistant, asking him, 'Is that an *a* or an *i*?' The assistant replies, '*a*'. The comedian reads on, 'The queen passed over the bridge.'

Many references to sex are covert or indirect. Oblique references to sex often have a certain cleverness that would be missing from direct reference. Freud claimed, 'The greater the disproportion between what is directly offered in the obscenity and what is necessarily aroused in the mind of the listener, the finer is the witticism and the higher it may venture in good society.' Certainly oblique references can be used in a greater range of situations and can avoid censorship. For many years there were humorous postcards sold in British seaside resorts, which often displayed a primary school level of crudeness. At least one was more adult, and quite naughty for its time. I guess it got past the censors because it did not mention anything naughty directly. It showed a woman asking the waiter to take back the watery jelly she had been served, with the words, 'Take this back. There are two things that I like to have firm, and one of them is jelly.'

Faced with a threat to his brain, Woody Allen cries, 'Oh, no, not my brain. That's my second favourite organ.' Someone says that sex isn't dirty. Woody replies, 'It is when you are doing it right.'

In the movie *Silver Streak* (1976) Gene Wilder meets the attractive Jill Clayburgh over dinner aboard the eponymous train. She tells him she is a secretary. He asks her about her skills. She confesses that her typing and shorthand are not up to scratch, so Gene asks her how she holds her job. 'I give great phone,' she replies.

There is an old joke about a wealthy, older man courting a young girl, who sought to discourage him by claiming her heart was already given to another. The man replied that he was not aspiring quite so high.

Another strategy is to sneak a sexual interpretation where none was intended. Once upon a time there was a formula for asking someone for a dance, 'May I have the pleasure of this dance?' It was often abbreviated to 'May I have the pleasure?' On one occasion a young man asked a young woman, 'May I have the pleasure?' to which she replied, 'No, but I'll dance with you.' Recently at a party the hostess offering hors-d'oeuvres to a guest used the formula 'May I tempt you to something?' He replied, 'No, but I'd love one of these chicken things.'

Traditionally certain words have been taboo to varying degrees. In the nineteenth century the word *damn* was considered pretty strong and not to be used by men in the company of women. The captain of Gilbert and Sullivan's *H.M.S.Pinafore* boasted that he never ever used 'the big D', well, hardly ever. Even in the middle of the twentieth century comedians were referring to Amsterdam as *Amsterdash*, though I suspect by then the naughtiness had all but evaporated. Over the course of the twentieth century a number of words have moved from the 'restricted' category into general use. These include words like *arse/ass*, *bastard*, *bloody*, *bugger* and *shit*. More recently *fuck* has been somewhat derestricted. It has been used in films since the 1980s and nowadays these f-words have been retained when the movies are shown on television. Of the traditional 'rude' words only the word *cunt* remains fairly strongly tabooed. It is used sparingly in films, but it is not normally allowed on television, though it did get aired in one episode of *Sex and the City*.

In Shakespeare's *Henry V* the French princess Katharine is enquiring about the English language from her maid, Alice. She asks what the English is for *le pied* and *la robe* and is embarrassed to learn that the English equivalents are 'foot' and 'gown' since 'foot' is very similar to the French f-word (*fut*) and 'gown' to the French c-word (*coun*).

The fascination with rude words of many people is amazing. Occasionally I've seen the L and the I joined in CLINT EASTWOOD or BILL CLINTON, and we've all lost count of the number of times we have seen the 'f-word' scrawled on a wall. There is also the practice of writing something that is close to a taboo word. I saw a young man wearing a T-shirt with the words *I want an FCK, all I need is U*. Currently we have the brand name *FCUK* on signs and on clothing. It stands for *French Connection United Kingdom*. And there is a movie *Meet the Fockers*. A few years ago Funk and Wagnall's ran a series of television ads for their dictionary, which ended with the slogan, 'Look it up in your Funk and Wagnall's'. Trying saying it!

Tongue-twisters are popular with children, and they were used by police for sobriety testing before the introduction of breathalysers. Try saying *The Leith police dismisseth us* if you are drunk. In fact, try saying it if you are sober. There is a tongue-twister designed to trap you into using the f-word:

I am a pheasant plucker, a pheasant plucker's son, And I'll be plucking pheasants till all the pheasant plucking's done.

And children have sentences like the following, which they ask you to say as quickly as you can, so they can laugh at your embarrassment when you discover you have spelt out the f-word.

If you see Kaye, tell her I'd like to see her.

Children also have expressions like the following, which you are invited to repeat with your index fingers pulling the corners of your mouth as far apart as possible.

Ride the bucking horse.

The following anecdote is authentic and highlights the pitfalls of using taboo words in front of children if you expect them to refrain from using them.

A respectable woman married a man much given to profanity. Even when their daughter was born, he couldn't curb his tongue, with the result that the little girl picked up rude words quite early in life, much to her mother's dismay. One day the child found the door slamming in her face and said, 'Bugger!'
'Don't say that,' said her mother. 'That's not nice.'
The daughter replied, 'What do you expect me to say when the bloody door slams?'

The fascination with matters rude is not confined to the English-speaking world, nor to Europe. There are numerous examples from various cultures, enough to suggest the interest is universal. Anthropologists and linguists from various continents report a variety of jokes centred on sex and bodily functions. For some societies, such as our own, any natural delight we take in sexually oriented humour is enhanced by the knowledge that such jokes annoy puritans. As evidence of how up-tight such puritans can be, witness the fact that in the 1930s an American band with six members had to be called a 'quintet', because 'sextet' would have been too suggestive.

Fiction would be practically impossible if humans refrained from fornication and adultery, and unfaithfulness figures prominently in humour. Henry (Henny) Youngman is quoted as saying, 'Some people ask the secret of our long marriage. We take time to go to a restaurant two times a week. A little candlelight, dinner, soft music and dancing. She goes Tuesdays, I go Fridays.' And I recall Groucho Marx quipping, 'We in the industry know that behind every successful screenwriter stands a woman. And behind her stands his wife.'

If you want to be entertained by humour, it doesn't do to be too uptight. The majority of jokes are sexually oriented, insulting to some group or other, or involve cruelty. Some jokes combine these characteristics. The joker wants you to suspend your moral principles for the purposes of appreciating the cleverness, assuming there is some, of course. Take the joke about the woman who hears a policeman knocking on the door when she is just out of the shower. 'I can't come to the door right now. I'm not dressed,' she says. 'I'm sorry, madam,' says the policeman, 'but your husband's been run over by a steamroller.' 'Oh,' says the woman, 'just slip him under the door.' Obviously, you have to ignore the tragedy this would be in real life and view it as you would the explosions in a Tom and Jerry cartoon.

For most sexually oriented humour, you usually need to suspend moral judgement, as in the following, where you are expected to chuckle at the unexpected revelation of the husband's naughtiness.

A couple got married, but they decided to put off having a family until they could afford a house. She left the birth control in his hands. One day she was surprised and

horrified to find that she had fallen pregnant. Her husband was at work, but she rang him immediately. As soon as he answered, she launched her attack, 'You've got me pregnant, you bastard.' There was a pause, then he replied, 'Who's calling, please?'

Insults

Trading smart insults is widespread across cultures, probably universal. In many small-scale, preliterate societies, 'joking relationships' are a feature of the communication between certain groups. One group in the relationship is expected to insult another or the two groups are expected to trade insults. Often the joking relationship is between kin, or between males and females who are potential partners. In ancient Greek and Roman society, in the European cultures that followed, and in Arabic culture, clever insults have been part of the stock-in-trade of the professional jester. In another variation there is an exchange of insults, as in the 'flytings' of the Scottish poets of the fifteenth and sixteenth centuries, where two poets would heap extravagant and outrageous abuse on one another, each trying to outdo the other in wit and imagination for the benefit of an audience. We now have the *poetry slam*, a competition in which poets compete on the basis of their poems and their delivery to an audience, but the poems are not normally directed against fellow poets. Some rap artists, however, attack fellow artists in the flyting tradition. We also have the *celebrity roast*, where a public figure is invited to dinner and professional comedians and others make fun of him or her.

This practice of exchanging insults is a feature of African-American culture, where it is known as 'the dozens' or 'doin' the dozens'. It can range from light-hearted banter to serious taunting. The themes are often sexual, and disparaging your opponent's mother or sister is common. In theory, such a slur is maximally insulting and a provocation to the insulted person to defend the honour of a mother or sister. But in practice such insults are often recognized as stylized and lacking in force through regular use, just as happens with *son-of-a-bitch* and *mother-fucker*. Examples include *Yo momma's like a screen saver, she's on everybody's laptop; Your mother's like a railroad track—laid all over the country;* and *Your mother's like a police station—dicks going in and out all the time.* These last two combine puns with colourful exaggeration, but most lines or 'snaps' rely just on exaggeration. The victim is expected to hit back and cap the insult with a stronger one. For instance, A might say, *Yo' momma's so old she was at Nazareth High when J.C. was there.* B might come back with *Yo' momma's so old she dated Moses in high school.* A has the last word with *Yo' momma's so old she baby-sat Adam.* Obesity is another subject for ridicule. A might use an old joke to start with, *Yo' momma's so fat, when she stepped on the scale it said, 'One at a time, please!'* B then has to go one better with something like *Yo' momma's so fat she entered Miss America and parts of Canada and Mexico.* Stupidity is another theme (*Yo' momma's so stupid that when someone said drinks were on the house, she went up on the roof*), as is ugliness (*Yo' momma's so ugly she frightens blind people*).

Exaggerated insults are not confined to African-American culture, nor even to the spoken mode of delivery. A lot of extreme insults are presented in lists and circulated as a type of joke. Many people will come across examples like the following in joke collections in books or magazines, or on websites, but never hear them used.

If your mother and father got divorced, would they still be brother and sister?

I've got a spare minute. Tell me everything you know.

You're so stupid, you told everyone that you were 'illegible' because you couldn't read.

You're so stupid, when you heard 90% of all accidents occur around the home, you went out.

You're so hairy it's best you steer clear of velcro.

It takes him one and a half hours to watch *60 Minutes* (or two minutes to play the Minute Waltz).

If you gave him a penny for his thoughts, you'd get change.

Traditional targets for insult tended to be obesity ('bum like the back of a bus'), pomposity and self-importance ('so far up himself that he needs a snorkel to breathe'), promiscuity of women [n.b.!] ('roots like a rabbit', where 'root' is an Australian colloquialism for 'intercourse' or 'have intercourse'), stupidity ('asked for his sushi well done'), under-endowment ('tits like warts', 'prick like a gherkin'), and alleged ugliness ('face like an old dartboard'). When I was at school and a smoker asked you, 'Have you got a match?' you replied, 'Yes, your face and my arse.' The targets for schoolkids' abuse include spoilsports, swots, dunces, copycats, show-offs, cowards, cry-babies, and tell-tales.

Trading insults is common among children, including the use of rhymes such as the following, which I remember from primary school.

Roses are red,
Violets are blue.
God made me beautiful,
But what happened to you?

When you were called names, you replied with the following rhyme.

Sticks and stones may break my bones,
But words will never hurt me.

Direct insults are common among children, but they are pretty much taboo among mainstream adults in most circumstances. However, young people often carry on the tradition of schoolyard badinage. Here is an example of verbal sparring from two young men who are getting dressed to go out for the evening.

A: What are you sprucing yourself up for? Do you think you're going to get lucky?
B: I might.
A: I don't think there're going to be any blind girls there.
B: You should talk. You look as if you're from the *Planet of the Apes*.
A: Better than being skinny like you. If you turn sideways, no one will be able to see you.

Sports players trade insults often to obtain an advantage by distracting or upsetting an opponent. In cricket this practice has been known for some time as *sledging*, but the term has been extended to other sports. The range of insults focuses on the lack of prowess of an opponent, or their lack of success on a particular occasion. Some of the insults sound trivial, but others are more serious, such as alleging that the addressee's mother or partner is promiscuous. However, in practice these tend to be treated like the stylized insults of the African-Americans illustrated above. The Australian wicketkeeper, Rod Marsh, once greeted the England batsman, Ian Botham, when he came in to bat with the words, 'How's your wife and my kids?' I'm sure Botham didn't take that too seriously.

Indirect insults can be particularly wounding to the victim (and more entertaining to third parties) if they appear to arise spontaneously, as in the following.

A: Excuse me. Are you a vet?
B: Yes. Are you ill?

Guest: Who is that very plain woman sitting by the door?
Host: That's my sister.
Guest: I'm sorry. I didn't notice the resemblance.

3

Where humour is to be found

I will begin by talking about where humour is NOT found. Humour is fun, and there are always puritanical types who are opposed to fun. In the Christian tradition there have been various influential voices denouncing humour or laughter. In Ephesians 5 : 3–4 it is written, 'Since you are God's people, it is not right that any matters of immorality or sexual indecency or greed should be even mentioned among you. Nor is it fitting for you to use language which is obscene, profane or vulgar.' One can see the wisdom of prohibiting 'dirty talk', since talking dirty or accepting dirty talk can signal availability. But some Church Fathers condemned humour more widely, and not surprisingly the rules of various religious orders have prohibited laughter. Some theologians pointed out that there is no record of Jesus Christ ever laughing, but I suspect Jesus was in fact a bit of a wit. His words 'Ye blind guides, which strain at a gnat and swallow a camel' (Matthew 23 : 24) involve a play on *galma* 'gnat' and *gamla* 'camel' in Aramaic. Likewise, there is some humour in the Old Testament. When God tells Abraham and Sarah that they are going to have a son, they laugh because such an event would seem to be impossible; as the Authorized Version delicately puts it, 'Now Abraham and Sarah were old and well stricken in age, and it ceased to be with Sarah after the manner of women.' Nine months later Sarah has a son, and they name him Isaac, which means 'laughs'.

In general, prohibitions on laughter have been confined to religious orders or to behaviour in church or courts of law or other places where one is expected to maintain an appropriate decorum.

Professional humour

Throughout European history there have been professional providers of humour. In the ancient world there were men who got themselves invited to banquets and provided entertainment. In the Middle Ages and later there were jesters at court and in the homes of the wealthy. These entertainers appear to have dealt largely in mimicry, parody, and insult. The nineteenth century saw the beginning of mass commercial humour with jokes, riddles and cartoons in newspapers and magazines, as well as comedians in music halls and variety shows.

Nowadays professional humour is abundant. There is a continual stream of comedy plays and movies, and television offers sit-coms, sketches and skits, and various types of show where the host provides humour.

Stand-up comedians are to be found in clubs and hotels, and also on television. Following tradition, many of them tell a string of short jokes, usually including topical ones. These are mostly old jokes recycled and adapted to apply to whatever is in the news, whether it be the death of Princess Di or, more recently, the marriage of Prince Charles and Camilla (Chas and Cas). The current trend with stand-up comedians is to relate incidents, real or imaginary, from their everyday life, usually ones where they are the victim.

The current fashion in newspapers, whether tabloid or broadsheet, is to include puns or other forms of word play in all but the more serious of headlines. Recent examples include an article on the Pope's ruling on celibacy for priests titled *Holy Orders*, an article on the banks refusing to accept large quantities of damaged coins headed *Coin Policy Makes No Cents*, and at the top of an article on the high cost of mobile phones *Talk Is Not Cheap*.

Word play is common in advertising, both in the names of businesses and in their slogans. A 'hamburger joint' is called *Lord of the Fries*, a Berlei bra 'Feels like it's *barely* there', and a TV drama series based in a plastic surgery clinic is called *Nip / Tuck*, playing on the expression '*nip and tuck*'. Numerous firms that provide bulldozers and back hoes promise 'that the earth will move for you' and one supplier of stones for landscaping invites people to 'get their rocks off' him.

Amateur humour

Outside professional ranks there are certain people who regularly tell jokes, and a large number of people who occasionally tell jokes. At workplaces, whether offices or factories, there are always jokes circulating, including topical ones, which presumably get picked up from professionals. Where people are relaxing outside work, say over drinks in a pub, it is normal for there to be humour, some of it the relating of humorous incidents and some of it in the form of jokes. In such a setting, one joke is likely to lead to another, with various participants trying to add to the merriment or perhaps trying to outdo the others. Nowadays a lot of jokes are circulated by e-mail. Some are copied from websites, where thousands of jokes are readily available.

A joke is a particular formal speech act. It is often introduced by a line such as 'Did you hear the one about the travelling salesman ...?' or it consists of a formula such as 'What do you get if you cross x with y?' But besides packaged jokes much humour can simply be slipped into dialogue by taking its cue from what was just said or from the situation. Puns are probably the most common such option. For instance, in *Diamonds Are Forever* (1971) James Bond is asked by a character called Leiter how some swallowed diamonds are to be recovered. 'Alimentary, my dear Leiter,' replies Bond, playing on what is generally thought to be a catch-phrase of Sherlock Holmes, namely, *Elementary, dear Watson* (a phrase Holmes never actually utters in Conan Doyle's stories). Here the reply answers the question, but contains a pun.

Incidentally, in most dialects of English *alimentary* and *elementary* are not pronounced exactly alike, but they are similar enough.

In a similar way humour based on ambiguous sequences can play a part in jokes or simply be the result of a spur-of-the-moment realization that what has been said can be given another twist. The following is a bit of dialogue I overheard between two men. We'll call them Wayne and Mark. Mark fancied himself as a bit of a wit.

Wayne: Debbie rang up to say she was pregnant.
Mark: She told you she got pregnant by phone?
Wayne: Yes.
Mark: And they say phone sex is the safest.

Some people are naturally witty and can easily manage to slip in a pun or drop in a clever allusion. Others interlard their speech with deliberate malapropisms (see Chapter 10). I knew someone who always spoke of the *sympathy orchestra* (symphony) and the *Bundaberg concertos* (Brandenberg). On his rare visits to church he would refer to the verger as the *virgin* and communion as *communication*. He also used expressions such as *since time immoral* (immemorial), spoke of a child who was a bad speller as *spelling like a witch*, and during the Cold War he would speak of Russians *defecating* to the West. Every mongrel dog was a *rottweiler–chihuahua* cross, and whenever someone mentioned sodomy, he would say, 'We know what they did in Sodom, but what did they do in Gomorrah?'

Others are ready to use standard, pre-made witticisms such as *effluent society* (affluent). If someone with an apparent aversion for physical work is mentioned, they will say *He thinks manual labour is a Spanish bullfighter*. If someone says, 'The dog's dug up thousands of my flowers', they will come in with *Haven't I told you a million times not to exaggerate?* If someone mentions Miss So-and-so, who taught them in primary school, she will be referred to as *My mistress at school. I had her in grade three*. To indicate that a certain letter is not pronounced, they will say *It is silent, like the 'p' in swimming*.

Most teachers and lecturers insert a few jokes to entertain their audience, and people making speeches are usually expected to include a joke or two, even if they are not normally given to being witty. This certainly applies to speeches at engagement parties, weddings, launches and openings, welcomes and introductions, and speeches at a function for someone retiring. At a funeral it is not uncommon to tell the odd humorous anecdote in the eulogy. When it comes to written humour, it is not always easy to distinguish the amateur from the professional. Most graffiti are amateur, but professional cartoonists and others have adopted the genre. Sometimes one comes across clever number (licence) plates. David Crystal in *Language Play* reports examples such as YRUILL 'Why are you ill?' registered to a doctor in the USA and IC2020 registered to an eye-doctor. T-shirts often carry humorous material.   In the early days of feminism T-shirts that read *Women on top* were popular.

Amateur and professional humour come together on the web. The internet has made it easy to circulate jokes and there are numerous sites featuring collections of jokes, some quotes from famous writers or professional comedians, others anonymous jokes that have been in circulation for years. Some are blatantly sexist and racist and appear to be amateur attempts at humour.

From time to time one encounters the odd witty sign, some unintentionally so. Outside the Nindigully pub in Queensland, there is one that reads *Free beer tomorrow*. When I first saw it, it raised my hopes for a moment or two until the penny dropped. Clothing shops often have signs such as *All our stock reduced*. I imagine these are serious and refer to the price not the size of the jackets and trousers, but the latter is a humorous possibility. There's a similar ambiguity with *Shirts just $15. They won't last*, which raises questions about the durability of the shirts. Worse still was the sign displayed outside a garage that had cheap tyres for sale: *Tyres slashed*. People often put up notices at their workplace, which tend to exhibit a cynical humour, as in *The light at the end of the tunnel has been turned off* or *Never put off until tomorrow what you can avoid altogether*.

It is common these days to send text messages via mobile phones. This encourages an imaginative use of brevity. So the office Romeo might send the object of his desire *U R QT* 'You are a cutie', to which she (or nowadays he) might reply *PO* 'piss off'.

4

Laughs in the lexicon

When we think of humour, we think of something new, something fresh at least, even if it turns out to be old material rehashed, but there are some witty expressions long established in the language. They might have struck people as clever or funny when they were first created, but they have become too familiar to engage our attention. Consider the word *butterfingers*, for instance. It refers to someone who lets a ball slip through the fingers when trying to catch it. You can use it as a derisive epithet when someone does this once, or you can apply it to someone who habitually drops catches. I suppose a term such as 'catch-dropper' could have been invented, but *butterfingers* shows more imagination. Clever and colourful terms are to be found mainly in the colloquial language. In fact, the main differences between the national and regional varieties of English, apart from accents, lie in the informal language, and countries and areas tend to be proud of their distinctive and colourful colloquialisms.

The lexicon is not static. New words are added from time to time, and a survey of recent additions reveals a lot about culture. Sometimes new words are borrowed from another language, as with *graffiti* (Italian), *genre* (French), *enchilada* (Mexican Spanish) and *tsunami* (Japanese), but more often they are made up using the resources of the existing language. Every language has rules for making up new words. In English the two common and traditional methods have been forming a compound of two words, as in *bookcase* or *cloudburst*, or using a prefix, as in *pre-school* or *defrost*, or a suffix, as in *tender-ize* or *film-dom*. Recently, however, the popularity of blending has increased dramatically. Blending involves taking part of one word and part of another to form a new word, as with *smog* (smoke + fog) or *brunch* (breakfast + lunch).

Compounds

A review of the compounds added to the language over the last forty years or so reveals a lot about changes in society. Think about well-known words such as *fast-track*, *role model*, *designated driver* and *designer dress*, and others not so well known such as *granny bank* 'grandparents as loan source to finance a major purchase such as buying a house for their children or paying school fees for their grandchildren', *identity theft* 'theft of personal details especially credit card numbers in order to commit fraud', and *face time* 'time spent talking face to face (usually to a client) as opposed to phone or e-mail communication'.

It is a feature of English that not all compounds are written as one word. There are in fact three possibilities. The components can be written as one word, they can be linked with a hyphen or they can be written as two separate words. In speech almost all compounds are distinguishable from a sequence of two words by the fact that a compound bears just one strong stress on its first word, but the fact that a compound can be written as separate words allows for humorous possibilities where an adjective precedes it. For instance, someone sees an advertisement for *odourless fly spray* and remarks, 'That would be handy if you've got odourless flies', and *amateur mouse poison* raises the possibility of professional mice.

Some of the newer compound words in English strike me as having a certain cleverness. These include *bad hair day* 'a day when nothing seems to go right', *glass ceiling* 'the invisible barrier that tends to prevent women being promoted to lofty levels', *granny dumping* 'putting grandma in the nursing home', *junk mail* 'unsolicited mail, whether hard copy in the letter-box or electronic mail', *mall rat* 'a youth who hangs around shopping malls', *mouse potato* 'someone who spends their leisure time in front of a computer' (derived from *couch potato*) and *snail mail* 'ordinary mail as opposed to e-mail'. The new compound *road rage* has provided the model for terms for numerous other kinds of rage. One I can relate to is *wrap rage*—the anger one feels when one cannot break into the packaging of one's purchases. Perhaps the smartest expression to be spawned by the computer age is *word of mouse* for news or information circulated by computer users. In the campaign for women to have more cubicles than men in public toilets the term *potty parity* has been coined. Note how *potty* (small child's po) is chosen to alliterate with *parity*. The term *dead cat bounce* refers to a small but insignificant rise following a large fall in the value of shares or whatever. The idea behind this term is that even a dead cat will bounce just a little bit when dropped.

Colloquial compounds are often the self-conscious result of attempts at humour, such as some of the recent creations for men's swimming briefs: *cluster busters, nutcrackers, penis poppers* and *slug-huggers*. Older examples of colloquial compounds include *brown tongue* and *brown nose* 'sycophant', *carrot-top* 'redhead', *flea-rake* 'comb', *nun's fart* 'cream-puff', *snot block* 'vanilla slice', *snot rag* 'handkerchief', *stickybeak* 'someone annoyingly inquisitive about what others are doing' and *underground mutton* 'rabbit'.

Blends

Two words can be blended to form one, as with *motel* (motor–hotel) and the colloquial, but well-established, *fantabulous* (fantastic–fabulous) and *ginormous* (gigantic–enormous). Disraeli said that old people often fall into *anecdotage*, cleverly combining *anecdote* and *dotage* to capture the notion that as old people fall into their dotage they are much given to telling anecdotes, particularly stories from their early life. Disraeli was ahead of his time. Blends were not particularly common in the nineteenth century, though Lewis Carroll contributed one or two including *chortle* from *chuckle* and *snort*.

As noted above, blending has become very popular over the last few decades. Normally the making up of new words is something the community is hardly aware of, but blending words together has become a kind of popular word game. The OED (revised second edition) includes two words for new breeds of dog: *labradoodle* and *cockapoo*. *Labradoodle* is a blend of *Labrador* retriever and *poodle*, a nice example in that the blended word refers to a blend of breeds. The same applies to *cockapoo*, a blend of *cocker* spaniel and miniature *poodle*, though the combination sounds like a rude word.

There are different ways of combining words. In some cases a whole word is combined with part of another, as in *vodkatini*, a blend of vodka and martini. In other cases there is overlap, as in *bagonize* 'to wait anxiously at the baggage carousel for the bags to arrive' or *baggravation*, what you feel when your bags don't arrive. *Affluenza*, 'the disease of being too rich' manages to keep the *fluens* part of both *affluence* and *influenza*. In *ambisextrous*, one letter (or sound) of *ambidextrous* is altered to yield *sex* sitting in the middle of *ambidextrous*.

The *Washington Post's* 'Mensa Invitational' runs an annual competition in which readers are asked to take any word from the dictionary, alter it by adding, subtracting, or changing one letter, and supply a new definition. Here are some of the winners for 2005:

Cashtration: The act of buying a house, which renders the subject financially impotent for an indefinite period.

Ignoranus: A person who's both stupid and an asshole.

Intaxication: Euphoria at getting a tax refund, which lasts until you realize it was your money to start with.

Foreploy: Any misrepresentation about yourself for the purpose of getting laid.

Giraffiti: Vandalism spray-painted very, very high.

Sarchasm: The gulf between the author of sarcastic wit and the person who doesn't get it.

Inoculatte: To take coffee intravenously when you are running late.

Decafalon: The gruelling event of getting through the day consuming only things that are good for you.

Caterpallor: The colour you turn after finding half a worm in the fruit you're eating.

Although these are formed by a change of letter, the results are blends of various kinds, some containing complete words and all combining two words. With the exception of *giraffiti*, which appears to have caught on, these are not new words in the language, but they are similar to others that are, and they illustrate the current widespread practice of making up smart blends. Among new blends that have some currency we find the following:

Chugger (charity + mugger) is a person who approaches people in the street to solicite donations.

Coca-colonization is the spread of American culture as represented by Coca-Cola.

Himbo (*he* or *him* plus *bimbo*) is a clever creation for 'male bimbo'.

Snaparazzi and *stalkerazzi* are clever variations of *paparazzi*, the former denoting an amateur paparazzo, and the latter, one who goes to lengths to track his celebrity target.

Metrosexual is very much in vogue at the time of writing for a man who is up with the latest fashion in dress, cuisine and lifestyle generally. It appears to be made up from *metropolitan* and *homosexual*, not that it implies homosexuality, though it does reflect the fact that a metrosexual's lifestyle is likely to raise the question. A man who doesn't care about his appearance and lifestyle is a *retrosexual*, which combines the prefix *retro-* with *(homo)sexual*.

Footbrawl (football + brawl) is a term for outbreaks of violence on the football field.

Greenwash (green + hogwash) refers to a corporation's superficial concern for the environment.

In 1972 supporters of President Nixon broke into the offices of the Democratic Party's National Committee at the Watergate Hotel in Washington. They were discovered and the name *Watergate* became synonymous with scandal. In 1986 the Reagan administration was found to have been selling arms to Iran and this was dubbed *Irangate*. The profits were being used to supply the anti-Communist Contra guerrillas in Nicaragua. This was *Contragate*. Soon every scandal was some kind of *-gate*. We had *pornogate* (someone slipped porno pictures into a magazine the Clintons were showing to children), *Dianagate* (Princess Di had a boyfriend), *Camillagate* (Prince Charles had a girlfriend) and when Monica Lewinsky went down on the president we had *zippergate* and *fornigate*. When Janet Jackson's breast got exposed accidentally on purpose during a performance at the Superbowl, the incident was dubbed *nipplegate*.

Brief swimwear and underwear has been the subject of some witty inventions. The *bikini* was named after Bikini Atoll in the Marshall Islands, the site of the first experimental atomic bomb explosions after World War II. The reason for the choice of name for the swimsuit is uncertain. Perhaps the effect of a shapely woman in such a brief swimsuit was thought likely to have an explosive effect on the male, or perhaps it was because of the danger of fallout. The *bikini* was followed by the *monokini* (top part missing), *seekini* (transparent bikini), *tankini* (tank top, bikini bottom), *camikini* (camisole top and bikini bottom) and *hikini* (high-cut briefs). These names are based on pretending that the first syllable of *bikini* is the prefix *bi-* 'two' as in *bicycle*. Another piece of swimwear or underwear that is well-named, though not just by blends, is the ultra-brief item that disappears between the buttocks. It has clever names in different parts of the world: *G-string* (because of its size), *thong* (because it fits between the buttocks the way the strap of a sandal fits between the toes) and *dental-floss bikini* (because it fits between the buttocks just like dental floss between adjacent teeth). The male G-string is a *banana hammock*.

Prefixes and suffixes

New prefixes or suffixes are rare, but a new prefix has appeared recently. It is *Mc-* , as in the McDonald's fast-food chain. The most widely used word to feature this prefix is *McJob*, which refers to a low-paid, insecure type of job with limited prospects for advancement. This reflects the impression many people have of employment with McDonald's. Whether the impression is justified is another matter and understandably McDonald's have objected to the entry in the eleventh edition of the *Merriam-Webster Collegiate Dictionary* (2003), where it is defined as 'low paying and dead-end work'. If this were the only *Mc*-word, we could consider it a blend, but in fact *Mc-* has caught on and is featured as a prefix in a number of other creations.

McGarbage: **waste from disposable dishes, cutlery and packaging.**

McGod: **the God of TV evangelists. There's also** *McTelevangelism.*

McMedicine: **a walk-in clinic in a retail environment where one gets quick treatment for routine ailments from nurses using computerized back-up for diagnoses. Prices are listed on a menu board (that's the bit I like). There's also** *McHealthcare.*

McMansions: posh, near-identical houses on a new housing estate.

McMovies: popular movies given a lot of publicity aimed at taking big profits on the first days of screening.

McPrisons: privatized prisons.

Presumably, the creators of these terms see an analogy with McDonald's, and one can see that they all have to do with a modern, efficient, convenient alternative aimed at a mass market (the McPrisons too?), but it is also true that they have derogatory connotations and apply to what many see as an inferior alternative to a traditional product or service.

Sometimes people try to be witty by treating prefixes or suffixes as words. In the musical *Camelot* there's a song 'The Merry Month of May' with a line 'every whim whether proper or *im-*', and Samuel Goldwyn is reported to have said on one occasion 'In two words: *im*-possible'.

One can also try to be funny by removing a prefix or suffix and exposing a form that doesn't occur on its own. Recently I heard someone say, 'If the soil is friable, let's fry it.' The following contrived example illustrates some of the humorous possibilities to be had by removing affixes.

Though my behaviour was peccable and my skin maculate from acne, my hair was kempt and my clothing shevelled, so I felt that I was quite couth.

The use of *couth* as an attempt to be smart is something I have heard two or three times, so one could imagine it catching on. There is an adverb *gingerly*, as in 'After the fall, she got up *gingerly*', but there is no corresponding adjective *ginger* with that meaning. However, I have now heard about half a dozen instances of sports commentators using the missing adjective, as in 'He's got up, but he's looking pretty *ginger*', so this too could catch on.

Euphemism

A lot of recent word-building has been to do with the creation of euphemisms, nice-sounding alternatives to existing expressions. Words for things that are unpleasant tend to acquire unpleasant connotations. This leads to a quest for fresh terms and thus to frequent lexical replacement. Euphemisms are to be found in domains such as killing, dying, disease and disability, the areas of mortal dread we mentioned at the end of the previous chapter as being so prominent in jokes. Euphemisms are also common with bodily functions, where we find expressions such as *pass water*, *go to the bathroom*, etc., and sex, where there are numerous expressions such as *sleep with* or *make love to* for sexual intercourse, which is itself a euphemism. One factor that can lead to euphemism is homophony with a rude word. The word *cock* can still be used in Britain for the male domestic fowl, despite the potential embarrassment of saying a word that sounds the same as a colloquialism for 'penis', but in the USA it has been replaced by *rooster*. Perhaps that is just as well. Where would *Red Rooster* be without it?

Over the past generation we have seen a move to institute politically correct (p.c.) language, language designed to be inclusive and to avoid offence. Where it is a matter of inclusion, for instance, not using 'he' to cover both sexes as in 'If a student hands in work late, he will be penalized', this does not provide opportunities for humour. But where attempts are made to avoid offence, it is a different matter. This activity is an extension of traditional euphemism and leads to a lot of word and phrase creation. For instance, people with some kind of physical disability were once called 'crippled' or 'handicapped', but more recently they have been referred to as *disabled*, then *differently abled* and later again as *physically challenged*. People with mental disability were once often called to as 'retarded', but nowadays they are *mentally challenged* or *people with learning difficulties*. Most of the euphemisms and politically correct terms are compounds, many of them like *mentally challenged* with a modifying adverb in *-ly*.

This use of euphemisms and politically correct language has engendered a backlash. Many people find the p.c. terms something to make fun of, something to parody. I often hear people using phrases such as *vertically challenged* for 'short (in height)' or *intellectually challenged* for 'unintelligent', with a certain relish that suggests they find them somewhat amusing. If someone mentions a 'rat-catcher', someone else is likely to add mockingly, 'Don't you mean *rodent exterminator*?' Some parody politically correct language by making up outlandish examples such as *differently hirsute* for 'hairy' or *differently pleasured* for sadomasochists. Sometimes it's hard to tell the serious examples from the parodies, as with *socially challenged* used to describe a recluse.

Some politically correct terms are misleading and inaccurate. *People with learning difficulties*, for instance, covers many people in the normal range who have difficulties in only certain areas of learning. Ironically, youngsters were not slow to pick up *learning difficulties* and to mock one another with phrases such as *You've got a bit of the LDs*, something to add to their vast collection of politically incorrect terms such as *spaso* and *vegie*. Another problem with politically correct terminology is the size of the creations: *visually challenged* involves replacing a basic word *blind* with six syllables.

There is a grim humour in the CIA's euphemistic expression *terminate with extreme prejudice* and the US Department of State's directive that the word 'killing' had to be replaced by *unlawful deprivation of life*, and something disturbing about the indirect language in a report on a hospital death that said *the patient failed to fulfil his wellness potential*.

Colourful language

Sometimes the term 'colourful language' is used as a euphemism for swearing, but here it refers to fancy language, language full of metaphors and similes. The terms **metaphor** and **simile** will remind some readers of their schooldays, when they were taught to pick out metaphors ('He is a tiger') and similes ('He is like a tiger') in texts, particularly poems, but metaphors and similes abound in everyday language. Sometimes they are attributable to a particular person, as with *A woman without a man is like a fish without a bicycle*, which was put into circulation by Irina Dunn, but usually they are anonymous.

Colourful language also demonstrates two other features that students of verse were meant to note: **alliteration**, as in *bible-basher, greedy guts* and *thunder thighs*, and **rhyme**. Whereas the formal language has a few rhyming expressions such as *brain drain* and *snail mail*, the colloquial language has *arty-farty* (or *artsy-fartsy*), *bum chum* 'male homosexual', *fake bake* 'suntan achieved by lamp or bottle', *gang-bang, gender bender* 'someone combining characteristics of both sexes', *lovey-dovey* and *tin grin*. This last refers to the wearing of braces on the teeth.

There's a saying that 'familiarity breeds contempt'. Certainly familiarity can dull our appreciation of clever expressions, but what is familiar to one group may not be familiar to another, particularly when we are dealing with the colloquial language. Among males the expression *He hasn't seen it for a while* is widely used of a man with a paunch, but I've seen it raise a smile when used in front of someone for whom it is a novelty.

Another interesting expression is *weak as nun's wee* used of tea, the theory being that urine from a virginal source would not be full-bodied. Someone whose behaviour is despicable is *lower than a snake's belly*, a tornado or a charging footballer is said *to go through like a dose of (Epsom) salts,* someone working hard under pressure is *flat out like a lizard drinking water.* Someone who has to keep getting up to answer enquiries at a counter or run up and down stairs might complain they are *up and down like a prostitute's pants*.

Some colourful expressions are based on an ambiguous word form, where one meaning fits in with one part of the phrase and another meaning with another part of the phrase. For instance, there is a colourful expression for a firm that charges high prices: *They charge like a wounded bull. Charge* in the sense of 'rush forward' fits with 'bull' and *charge* in the sense of 'demand a high price' fits with 'they' (the firm, shopkeepers or whoever). Other examples of this kind of thing include *going like last week's pay, staying like a mother-in-law* and *having more push than a revolving door*. Someone who is aggressively competitive can be described as *someone who goes into a revolving door behind you but comes out ahead of you.*

Bodily functions and sexual activities probably attract most colourful expressions. Men have a number of 'humorous' expressions for urination, for instance, such as *splash the boots* and *drain the spuds.*

There are numerous 'colourful' expressions for mental disability such as *a shingle short, one brick short of a load* and *not playing with the full deck.* There's also *not the full quid* and *two bob short in the pound*, which are interesting too in that they preserve references to obsolete units of currency, namely the pound, which was known colloquially as the 'quid', and the shilling, known colloquially as a 'bob'. These terms also reflect a traditional unsympathetic view of mental illness, as does the old term *giggle-house* for what was once known officially as a lunatic asylum. Someone who is erratic is *silly as a two-bob watch*, an expression that relates to the cheap, unreliable watches introduced towards the end of the nineteenth century.

Meanness is another subject that gives rise to a number of expressions. A mean man can be called a *scrooge* after Ebenezer Scrooge in Dickens's *A Christmas Carol*, or can be said *to have deep pockets*, the implication being that he finds it difficult to reach down and extract money to pay for drinks or whatever when it is his turn.

Food seems to have come in for a fair share of derogatory metaphors. These include *doorstep* 'unduly thick slice of bread', *rabbit food* 'lettuce, salad', *frog spawn* 'sago' and *fly cemetery* 'currant cake'. Some years ago, when I was in London, 1979 to be exact, I noticed carafes of Australian wine for sale bearing the rubrics *Kanga Rouge* and *Wallaby White*. Not much good for the image of Australian wine, but clever use of language.

The 'Yellow Press' has often been a common source of colourful language, particularly sections dealing with the turf, where jockeys are *postillions*, whips *persuaders* and bookmakers *satchel swingers*. Sports broadcasters often use phrases full of colourful exaggeration. One Australian race broadcaster would describe horses who finished back in the ruck as 'seeing more tales than

Hoffman', if they pulled hard, they 'pulled like a dentist', and if they ran wide throughout a race, they were adjudged to have 'covered more ground than the early explorers'. A Melbourne football commentator uses frequent malapropisms for effect. For instance, he speaks of a player 'transvestiting the centre with a raking pass'.

Names

There can be cleverness and humour in names. Sometimes people have 'meaningful' names such as *Tom Katz* or *Anita Lay*, though it is uncertain whether these are genuine or made up. People in show business often adopt catchy names, as with the Hollywood actor *Rip Torn*. The rock star *Chubby Checker* took a name that is a 'translation' of *Fats Domino*, the name of a blues star of the previous generation.

It may happen that people find themselves in roles that fit their names: a few years ago the archbishop of Manila was *Cardinal Sin*; and a director of transport for the Inner London Education Authority was called *Rick Shaw*.

Comic literature abounds with funny made-up names, many of them rude. The subtitle of Gilbert and Sullivan's *The Mikado* is *The Town of Titipu*, and the characters include *Nanki-Poo* and *Pooh-Bah*. The main character in the comic strip *Blondie* was called *Dagwood Bumstead*.

Public figures sometimes receive clever nicknames. Jackson Pollock was dubbed *Jack the Dripper* because of his technique of dripping paint onto his canvases, and President Richard Nixon was widely known as *Tricky Dicky*. The athlete Florence Griffith-Joyner had the catchy nickname of *Flo-Jo*, and the US baseballer Howard Johnson was dubbed *Ho-Jo*. One Australian footballer, who is reluctant to release the ball to a teammate, has been dubbed *the pope* (he won't pass the pill).

The names of registered animals are often clever. Take racehorse names, for instance. The famous American horse *Sea Biscuit* was by *Hard Tack* and the not-so-famous Australian horse *Bobbitt* was out of *Cutter Girl* (in a much-publicized incident Mrs Bobbitt cut Mr Bobbitt's penis off. The severed organ was subsequently reattached and Mr Bobbitt became a celebrity). It is common to combine elements from the names of the sire and dam. The famous English steeplechaser *Red Rum* was by *QuoRUM* out of MaRED, and *Camilla's Beau* was by *Casual Lies* out of *Royal Infatuation*. In racing countries the names are controlled by a central authority, such as Weatherby's in Britain or the Jockey Club in the USA, and the restrictions include a ban on names that are vulgar, obscene or insulting. However, this ban is frequently put to the test. Recent names of dubious taste include *Haditovski*, *Stonun* (no nuts backwards—the horse was a gelding) and *Richard Cranium*.

5

Puns

Basic puns

As mentioned in Chapter 1, puns are the most common basis for humour. Bergson, the much-quoted author of *Le Rire* [*Laughter*] considered puns the least reputable form of humour. Freud wrote that they 'are generally counted as the lowest form of wit, perhaps because they are "cheapest" and can be formed with the least effort.' Oliver Wendell Holmes called punning 'verbicide'. Walter Redfern, on the other hand, devoted a whole book to the topic and wrote that 'it [the pun] can make an individual, like Hemingway's fortunate heroine, feel the ground move beneath. It can ruin lazy expectations, subvert the nature of language and thought.'

As noted in Chapter 1, a particular word form can have more than one meaning. Sometimes this is the result of accidental homophony. Homophones are words that happen to sound alike. Examples include *fin/Finn*, *seen/scene* and *profit/prophet*. There is a competing term **homonym**, but it is more accurately used as a cover term for **homophones** and **homographs** (words spelled alike). Two words can be both homophones and homographs as with *bear* (the animal) and *bear* (carry, tolerate).

The other way we finish up with a particular form having more than one meaning is from a word or phrase developing an extra meaning, often a metaphorical one. A word or phrase with more than one meaning is said to be polysemous. The word *mole* refers to a small burrowing animal (which makes molehills, not mountains), but it has also come to mean 'a spy employed in an organization', since the spy can be seen as burrowing unseen in search of information. Whether it is a matter of two separate roots happening to be pronounced alike or a particular word developing different meanings, the result is the same: one form has more than one meaning. Occasionally one encounters people who regret the existence of homophones and words with more than one meaning, but in practice this causes little ambiguity in context, and it has the advantage of making puns possible.

As far as I can tell, all languages allow for the possibility of puns, though the number of possibilities must vary from one language to another and over time. Modern French has a large number of homophones because it has lost so many word-final consonants. English too has quite a large inventory. Using a sample from a dictionary, I calculated that English has nearly 4000 homophonous pairs. One of the best examples can be found under *butt*. There is (1) thick end, (2) object of ridicule, (3) cask, (4) the verb *butt* 'to strike with the head'. Throw in the conjunction *but* and you have ten homophonous pairs, though admittedly it is hard to use the conjunction *but* in puns. Puns are normally between two members of the same part of speech, i.e. noun to noun, verb to verb or adjective to adjective, though Shakespeare manages to play on the noun *art* and the verb *art* in *Romeo and Juliet*, Act II, scene iii: ... *art thou what thou art, by art as well as by nature* ... The noun *butt* listed above as 'thick end' is polysemous and includes the butt of a tree, the butt of a cigarette, and the buttocks. Leaving aside the conjunction *but*, we have effectively six words that sound alike and therefore fifteen pairs of possible puns.

Counting substantially different meanings of words and phrases as separate, I found on the basis of a dictionary sample that polysemy could provide about another 4000 possibilities for punning. For example, I counted *shady* 'dark' and *shady* 'disreputable' as one possibility, *babbler* 'a person who babbles' and *babbler* 'type of bird' as another. The number would have been higher if I had made finer distinctions of meaning. In some instances, it was necessary to look at homophones and polysemes together, as with *butt* above. I included only those few proper names that occurred on the pages I sampled, but each person will know perhaps some thousands of proper names not included in the dictionary. These include names of famous people and places plus names of friends, acquaintances and places near where one lives. I did not count homophony between words and phrases (*attack/a tack*, *I lean/ Eileen*), though I did count polysemy in phrases such as the literal and metaphorical meanings of a phrase such as *pull in one's horns*. The exact figure is, of course, of no importance. All that is relevant is the fact that the number of possibilities for punning is very high.

Puns can be found in many literatures, and it is reasonable to assume they occurred in the thousands of languages, past and present, for which we have no record. Up till a few centuries ago serious puns were not uncommon, at least in literature. In Shakespeare's *Romeo and Juliet* Act III, scene i the dying Mercutio says, 'Ask for me tomorrow and you shall find me a grave man.' He also says the more quotable 'A plague o' both your houses.' In *The Merchant of Venice* (Act IV, scene i) Antonio makes a grim pun about the fact that he will die if Shylock actually cuts a pound of flesh from him,

**For if the Jew do cut but deep enough,
I'll pay it presently with all my heart.**

Shakespeare makes much use of puns, both serious and comic. He frequently puts them into the mouths of his 'low' characters, his working-class characters if you like. In *Julius Caesar* (Act I, scene i), for instance, a cobbler says that he is 'a mender of bad soles' and that he meddles 'with no tradesman's matters, nor women's matters, but with awl'. Here the pun is between *with awl* [a tool for making holes] and *withal* [besides] with the further reference to his tool being used (or not used) for women's matters, by which we are to understand sexual matters.

Puns can be the basis for recognized jokes (see Chapter 7), but they can also be introduced into normal speech or writing. On one occasion I was at a meeting, where the fortunes of those who had left the university were being reviewed. It was revealed that a certain Paul Ossa had left to open a restaurant. One wag asked whether he intended to offer Ossa Buco. On another occasion I heard a woman talking about what kind of carpet she was going to have in the house she and her husband had just bought. 'I'm going to have a berber in the lounge,' she said. To which someone added, 'And I suppose you'll have a shag in the bedroom.' This pun involves homophony between *shag* 'a type of rough carpet' and *shag* 'sexual intercourse', but plays on the polysemy of *Berber* (a North African ethnic group) and *berber* (type of carpet named after that group).

A subtle type of pun one occasionally comes across is the 'eye pun', which works on a pair of words that are spelled alike (homographs), but not pronounced alike. I once overheard two scholars in Hereford Cathedral admiring the stained-glass (or leaded) windows. One, quoting Milton's *Il Penseroso*, noted that they were *casting a dim religious light*. The other replied, 'Is that why they sing the hymn *Lead, kindly light*?' However, to make the pun he pronounced *lead* as *led*. There is an old joke based on the homography of *lead* (the verb) and *lead* (the noun): *You can lead a horse to water, but a pencil must be lead.*

Occasionally one encounters a 'rally' of puns where one pun stimulates punning repartee, a phenomenon sometimes referred to as 'ping-pong punning'. Here is an example from my local tennis club, which I remember (with advantages) from my youth. Barry is reading Tennyson (a set text for year 12) when Michael approaches.

Michael: Like a bit of tennis, son?
Barry: I'm game.
Michael: Well, if you've got the balls.
Barry: I have, so we are all set.
Michael: For an even match.
Barry: Should be rally good.

Repartee involving puns and word play often contains a sexual element where the aim is not only to show one's verbal skill, but to flirt, to test the partner's attitude, perhaps to elicit an invitation. The following is an amalgamation of two separate exchanges.

> She: I want to hang this picture somewhere around here.
> He: (tapping on the wall) You'll need to find a stud.
> She: I was hoping you would help.
> He: I'll give you my awl.
> She: That augers well.
> He: (after making a hole in the wall with the awl) There, now you've got a decent sort of hole.
> She: So all I need is a decent sort of screw.

Banter (or raillery or chaff) involves the exchange of word play with a teasing or provoking element. A sustained example occurs in Shakespeare's *The Taming of the Shrew* (Act II, scene i). Here are two excerpts. Petruchio, the suitor, is chatting up Katherine, the antagonistic shrew of the title, and seeks to introduce sex into the conversation at every opportunity. In this first excerpt Katherine calls him a moveable, a piece of furniture, in particular, a stool, so Petruchio asks Katherine to sit on him. He then picks up her use of *bear* (a load) with a pun on *bear* (children).

> Pet: Myself am moved to woo thee for my wife.
> K: Mov'd! in good time; let him that mov'd you hither
> Remove you hence: I knew you at the first,
> You were a moveable.
> Pet: Why, what's a moveable?
> K: A joint-stool.
> Pet: Thou hast hit it: Come, sit on me.
> K: Asses are made to bear, and so are you.
> Pet: Women are made to bear and so are you.

A few lines later Katherine warns Petruchio that she is a wasp with a sting. Petruchio points out that a wasp has its sting in its tail and he suggests an interesting way of removing it.

Pet: Come, come, you wasp; i' faith you are too angry.
 K: If I be waspish, best beware my sting.
Pet: My remedy is then to pluck it out.
 K: Ay, if the fool could find it where it lies.
Pet: Who knows not where a wasp doth wear his sting?
       In his tail.
 K: In his tongue.
Pet: Whose tongue?
 K: Yours, if you talk of tails; and so farewell.
Pet: What, with my tongue in your tail?

Puns are very common in the headlines of articles in newspapers and magazines. An article on slimming was headed *Waist disposal*, an article on the job dissatisfaction of long-haul airline crews was entitled *Long haul a real drag*, and a travel writer's dissatisfaction with what Frankfurt had to offer was called *Frankfurt: it could be wurst*.

Some parts of the lexicon seem just to be made for punsters. They include *animal husbandry*, *free radicals*, the poet *Longfellow* and the common verb to *come*, which can refer to sexual climax, and is only too easy to use ambiguously. The seventh planet from the sun has the name *Uranus*, which is homophonous with 'your anus' and the basis of innumerable jokes such as,

I've got a telescope. Would you like to look at Venus?
Yes, as long as I don't have to look at Uranus.

Cricket terminology is a fertile field for punsters, but the ambiguous word forms are so obvious that this is something you pick up at primary school. Some of the positions in the field have curious names such as *silly point*, *fine leg* and *long on*, all crying out for puns, and other positions include *the slips*. There is *first slip*, *second slip* and *third slip*. If the ball carries from the bat into the hands of one of the *slips* fieldsmen, one is said to be *caught in slips*, which has connotations of cross-dressing, since the form *slip* can refer to a petticoat. If a bowler bowls a set of deliveries (an over) from which the batsman scores no runs, he is said to have *bowled a maiden over*. This can be a source of great hilarity for twelve-year-olds, but is too obvious to be a source of mature humour. The term *maiden* is also used for animals that have not won a race: racehorses, harness horses, dogs, camels and whatever other animals are used in races. I recently heard a turf commentator talk of a horse 'coming straight to town after picking up a short maiden at Pakenham'.

The use of *balls* for 'testicles' provides another fertile ground for puns. Besides the legitimate activities that make up a game of cricket, there is sometimes the intrusion of a male streaker who will hurdle the stumps and run down the wicket. On one such occasion the commentator described the incident in the same, dry style he used for the game, saying, 'Those last two balls went very close to leg stump' and 'They're getting quite a lot of swing from the pavilion end'.

There are numerous synonyms for anything to do with sex or bodily functions and effluvia, including the toilet. So we have scores of words for 'things' such as breasts, penis, vagina, intercourse and prostitute. Breasts, for instance, can be called *tits, titties, boobs, jugs* or *mammaries*. Penis, for example, can be referred to by terms such as *cock, dick, roger, prick, dong, lance, rod, pole, horn, poker, shaft, stick, sword, dagger, sausage, tool* and *boner*. There is a story that *boner* derives from a belief that arousal results in a bone extending from the pelvic area and supplying the necessary firmness of purpose. There are also a few Yiddish terms such as *schlong*. In the film *When Harry Met Sally* Meg Ryan relates stories of the prowess of her lover to Billy Crystal, leading him to dub the lover *Wonderschlong*.

The words for vagina include the rather off-putting *box, crack, doughnut, slit, slot*, and *snatch*, plus more user-friendly 'soft and furry' terms such as *pussy* and *beaver*, though the latter may not derive directly from the furry dam-builder but from *beaver* in the sense of 'beard', itself derived from the name of the animal. The word *snatch* as a noun can also refer to a type of lift in weightlifting. A commentator was responsible for the following, apparently accidental, pun, 'This is Gregoriava from Bulgaria. I saw her snatch this morning and it was amazing.'

Intercourse can be referred to by words such as *bang*, *plough* and *screw*, as well as euphemisms such as *lie with*, *sleep with* and *go to bed with*. Since all of these synonyms, whether metaphorical or euphemistic, for the 'naughty parts' and what can be done with them retain their original meaning in almost all cases, they provide a fertile field for ambiguity.

Making a pun involves seeing a meaning not intended in the context. Sometimes it happens that a word occurs in a context where an unintended meaning arises accidentally. The word *bitch* refers to a female dog, but it is also used for a spiteful female, or just as a general not-too-complimentary term for females. Recently I heard a man say, 'I had a dozen bitches wanting a crack at him just this week.' Out of context, this sounds strikingly rude, but the speaker was the owner of a prize-winning male greyhound. A student writing about Lawrence's *Sons and Lovers* produced an accidental pun when she noted that *Mrs Morel was jealous of Paul's attachments*. No error there, but the choice of words has echoes of penis envy.

Some puns are made possible by the fact that certain verbs can be used in either an active or a quasi-passive sense. The verb 'to smoke', for instance, can be used to indicate an act of smoking (e.g. a cigarette) or the process of giving off smoke.

The doctor examines the female patient and then asks her, 'Do you smoke after having intercourse?' The woman replies, 'I don't know. I've never looked.'

A: Your dog looks as if he's had extensive surgery.
B: Yes, the vet had to cut off his nose.
A: But how does he smell?
B: Terrible.

Prostitutes appeal to priests.
Priests appeal to bishops.

As noted above, puns depend on accidents of homophony and the development of polysemy. The development of polysemy in one language may be matched by a parallel development in another, which would mean that some puns based on polysemy could be translated into another language, but puns based on homophony are normally not translatable. However, where words are borrowed from one language to another, a punning possibility may be transferred. There is a traditional story about Gregory (later Pope Gregory the Great), who saw some boy slaves from Britain and was told they were Angles. He replied, 'That is appropriate for they have angelic faces.' This play on words transfers from Latin to English since *Angles*, the name of the Germanic 'tribe', was borrowed into Latin as *Angli*, and the Latin word *angelus* (originally from Greek, plural *angeli*) was borrowed into English. Incidentally, a widespread apocryphal version of this story has Gregory saying, *Non Angli, sed angeli* 'Not Angles, but angels'. Not accurate, but the point is the same.

Here are a few more puns. This batch contains puns involving just a single word rather than a phrase.

Margaret Dumont: You remind me of my youth.
Groucho Marx: He must be quite a big boy by now.

Condoms should be used on every conceivable occasion.

We couldn't get any water until we'd pressed the minister.

The Human Cannonball wanted to retire from the circus, but the manager begged him to stay (obviously he didn't want to fire him!), because he knew it would be hard to find another man of his calibre.

The first thing that strikes you in Rome is the traffic.

The following example is adapted from Charles Lamb.

An Oxford scholar met a porter carrying a hare down Broad Street and asked him if it was his own hare or a wig.

Puns across word boundaries

So far the puns presented have been based on single words, but there can also be puns that run over word boundaries. One of the cleverest puns of this type, I think, was the motto linguists adopted at a conference in the USA. Because linguists use an asterisk to mark ungrammatical sentences, the motto emblazoned on hundreds of T-shirts at this particular conference was *Be ungrammatical. You only have your ass to risk.*

Here are a few more examples where the pun runs over a word boundary:

When you've seen one shopping centre you've seen a mall.

With her marriage she got a new name and a dress.

A vulture boards an airplane, carrying two dead raccoons. The stewardess looks at him and says, 'I'm sorry, sir, only one carrion allowed per passenger.'

Two boll weevils grew up in Arkansas. One went to New York and became a famous actor. The other stayed behind in the cotton fields and never amounted to much. He became known as the lesser of two weevils.

Puns involving phrases

The examples above involve homophony or near homophony across a word boundary. The next set of examples involves ambiguity of idiomatic phrases. In Hemingway's *For Whom the Bell Tolls*, the protagonist Robert Jordan asks his lover, Maria, whether she has reached climax with the words 'Did the earth move for thee?' This phrase has caught on and figures in numerous jokes (and ads for earth-moving firms). At one time Gough Whitlam, a former prime minister of Australia, and his wife, Margaret, had to be evacuated from a hotel in China during the night because of an earthquake. One cartoon showed them standing in the street in their dressing-gowns with Gough asking Margaret, 'Did the earth move for you too?'

Here are a few more examples where an idiomatic phrase is involved.

Feeling ecumenical, a Catholic priest invited a Protestant parson to the presbytery for afternoon tea. The parson was very impressed by the commodious dwelling with its fine furniture and fittings. 'My word,' he said. 'You priests do yourselves proud.' 'Yes,' said the priest. 'You may have the better halves, but we have the better quarters.'

John said he wouldn't mind a bit if conscription were introduced. Bill said he wouldn't mind a bit whether conscription was introduced or not.

Harry and Suzie used to meet at a nudist camp. At first they were keen to meet every weekend, but after a while they felt they were seeing too much of each other.

Police station toilet stolen. Cops have nothing to go on.

After the meeting of The Society for the Propagation of the Faith, Father Flynn asks Sister Anna whether he can walk her back to the convent. 'Just this once,' she says, 'but you mustn't get into the habit.'

Bakers trade bread recipes on a knead-to-know basis.

A truck driver saw an attractive woman thumbing a ride so he picked her up. In the course of conversation she told him she was a witch. He didn't believe her, but when she put her hand on his knee, he turned into a lay-by.

A boiled egg is hard to beat.

The next example is an old joke, but it is a clever one with three separate word puns worked into a phrase.

Three brothers bought a ranch in Texas and planned to raise cattle. They couldn't think of a name for their ranch so they asked their mother, who said, 'You should name it *Focus*.' The brothers were puzzled. 'Why?' they asked. 'Because,' said their mother, '*Focus* is where the sun's rays meet.'

Cross-language puns

Up to this point the puns have been between forms within the one language, but puns can be across languages. Once I was with a group in a restaurant when one member of the group was served some rather green-looking potato. An English chap in the group tried to dissuade him from eating the dubious potato, but someone else enjoined him to go ahead with the words 'Don't let a Pom deter you.' A *Pom* is an English person and *pomme de terre* (apple of earth) is French for 'potato'.

In her Christmas message of 1992 Queen Elizabeth, who had suffered a fire in Windsor Castle and a number of family embarrassments, said that she had had an *annus horribilis*, which is Latin for a 'horrible year'. One of the British tabloids ran the headline **One's bum year.** This is a clever piece of irreverence. It plays on the similarity between *anus* and *annus*, the former an English word (though taken from Latin) and the latter a Latin word, and it takes the form *bum*, more or less a synonym for *anus*, and uses the form as the colloquial adjective meaning 'bad', and then puts this together with the very formal *one's*, a form much in the mouth of the queen but not in that of most of her subjects.

Here are a few more examples:

When you're swimming in the creek, and an eel bites your cheek, that's a moray! [Dean Martin song 'That's Amore']

In reading the next example remember that *Juan* is pronounced like 'one'.

> **A woman has identical twins and gives them up for adoption. One of them goes to a family in Egypt and is named Ahmal. The other goes to a family in Spain, and they name him Juan. Some years later, Juan sends a picture of himself to his birth mother. Upon receiving the picture, she tells her husband that she wishes she also had a picture of Ahmal. Her husband responds, 'They're identical twins! If you've seen Juan, you've seen Ahmal!'**

Substituting a similar word

Besides puns that involve one particular form with more than one meaning, there are what we might call quasi-puns, half-puns or **paronyms**, where an expected word in a common expression or quote is replaced by a similar word, usually a rhyming one. There is a story of a man who was going to buy his wife her favourite anemones on the occasion of her birthday. However, he was held up at work and reached the florist's just before closing, only to find that they were sold out. All they had were some fern leaves. The man thought they looked rather nice, certainly better than nothing, so he bought some of these and presented them to his wife. 'With fronds like these,' she said, 'who needs anemones?'

Here are some other examples.

> **Shotgun wedding: a case of wife or death.**

> **When you dream in colour, it's a pigment of the imagination.**

> **Joe came back from his vacation with a terrible sunburn. His friend John took one look at his red skin and said, 'You certainly got what you basked for.'**

> **The Buddhist monk refused Novocaine during root-canal work because he wanted to transcend dental medication.**

6
Grammatical ambiguities

Interpreting a sentence involves taking each word to be a certain part of speech (for instance, noun or verb) and assigning some kind of structure to the sequence. However, it can happen that a certain sequence of nouns, verbs or what have you can be assigned more than one structure, and the would-be comedian is not slow to exploit this. In Chapter 1 an example of an ambiguous sequence contained the set-up *My mother made me a homosexual* and the punchline *If I sent her the wool, would she make me one too?* The sequence that formed the basis of the joke could be taken to mean either 'X made something for Y' or as 'X made Y to be something'. Here is another example of much the same ambiguity, which is from W. S. Gilbert (of Gilbert and Sullivan fame).

> **Stranger: Hey, you!**
> **Gilbert: Eh? You talking to me, sir?**
> **Stranger: Yes, you. Call me a cab.**
> **Gilbert: Certainly. You're a four-wheeler.**
> **Stranger: How dare you, sir! What do you mean?**
> **Gilbert: Well, you asked me to call you a cab, and I certainly couldn't call you** *hansom.*

The sequence *call me a cab* can be taken as 'Summon a cab for me' or it can be taken in the same way as 'Call me Kim.'

It is easy to produce a grammatical ambiguity unwittingly. The following sentence from a news report is quite grammatical, but it can be read in two opposite senses.

The USA does not want to get rid of Saddam Hussein, only to have him replaced by another dictator.

The problem is not just the word *only*. Even substituting *just* or *merely* leaves the ambiguity. A different construction is needed to avoid the problem.

Which part of speech?

In English many words can be used as more than one part of speech. The word *free*, for instance, can be an adjective in 'free love' or a verb in 'free the prisoner'. This ambivalence can be the basis for humour, as in a sequence such as *free agents*. Many word forms can appear as verbs or nouns, e.g. *run* can be a verb as in *I will run down the street* or a noun as in *I will go for a run*. In normal English words like *the* or *a* point to the presence of a following noun, and auxiliary verbs such as *will* or *may* point to a following verb, but these clues are often missing in headlinese and in the abbreviated text of ads, particularly classified ads. Sometimes inflections help sort out whether a word is a noun or a verb. For example, the *–ed* in *tapped* makes it clear that the root is the verb *tap*, not the related noun nor *tap* in the sense of 'faucet'. However, *–s* or *–es* can mark the plural of nouns (*He made many runs*) or occur with verbs (*He runs*), so it is no help.

Consider the following headline,

Toyota exports rocket.

Export can be a noun or a verb, and the *–s* on the end is no help in determining which it is, and *rocket* can be a noun or a verb. Is Toyota exporting a rocket? Or is it that Toyota exports have increased dramatically? Presumably it is the latter, but the sentence is ambiguous.

Here are a few more headlines where there is a problem with words that could be one part of speech or another. The choice then determines how you group the words, that is, how you construe the sentence.

Thief found safe in office.

British left waffles on Falkland Islands.

Church wants men to help lay women.

Eye drops off shelf.

Lawyers give poor legal advice.

Left turns out.

Man wanted to kill the king.

Paramedics help spider bite victim.

Nurses needed to help stroke patients.

Women lay preachers at Anglican Synod.

Cancer in women mushrooms.

The next example, not a headline this time, is trickier. One is fooled into interpreting the second sentence as parallel with the first, and then one discovers that that makes no sense.

Time flies like an arrow. Fruit flies like a banana.

A number of ambiguous sequences involve personal names, particularly surnames. These are distinguished in writing by a capital letter, but many names are homophonous with ordinary adjectives or verbs, from which they were derived in most cases.

Examples of 'ambiguous' names include *Black*, *Hyde*, *Purves*, *Standing*, *Suckling*, *White*, *Wilde* and *Wynne*.

Isn't that Dick Green?

I saw Sally Wynne.

I knew John Wood.

The *-ing* form of a verb is useful to the jokesmith. A word like *entertaining*, for instance, can be a participle of the verb *entertain* and take an object (*entertaining them*) or it can be an adjective and qualify a noun (*entertaining repertoire*). This means that sequences of *-ing* forms plus a following noun can provide further grouping ambiguities.

They wanted to see Morris dancing, but only managed to see Fred making a fool of himself.

'Do you like bathing beauties?'
'I don't know. I've never bathed any.'

Court to try shooting defendant.

Emergency service personnel worked around the clock monitoring river levels and flooding roads.

In the next example the *-ing* form of the verb is of the type sometimes called a gerund. The problem is whose drinking is to be stopped?

The vice-chancellor is going to stop drinking on campus.

Tigers who eat people, whether women or men, are called man-eaters. In the next example the word *eating* is a participle, but there is a grouping problem. Do we have a man-eating tiger or do we have a man with a more than healthy appetite?

Hunters catch man eating tiger.

Scope

In almost every sentence there is a nucleus consisting of a verb indicating an action or process and some nouns representing who or what is involved. Outside the nucleus there may be some more peripheral material indicating the time or place of the action, or the instrument used to carry out an activity and so on. In the following examples the periphery is shown in italics.

Birds fly *through the mist without any trouble*.
***Yesterday* Jane saw Fred *down the street*.**
***In January* Michael gave a donation to the tsunami appeal *from his winnings*.**

It is not always clear what the scope of these peripheral words and phrases is. Consider the sentence *The woman saw the man with the telescope*. This is ambiguous. It's a question of the scope of the phrase *with the telescope*. Does it apply to the *woman* or to the *man*? The more natural interpretation is that the woman used the telescope to see the man, but it could be she happened to see a man who had a telescope. There's a story of a woman who walked into a dress shop and asked the shop assistant, 'May I try on that dress in the window?' 'Wouldn't you be more comfortable in the fitting room?' replied the shop assistant. And there's an old Groucho Marx joke where he says, 'Did I ever tell you about the time I shot an elephant in my pyjamas? How he got into my pyjamas I'll never know.' Here the phrase 'in my pyjamas' should go with 'I', but it is placed at the end of the sentence and therefore looks as if it goes with 'elephant'.

With these examples in mind consider the source of ambiguity in the following:

Builders refuse to work after death.

Complaints about old people growing nasty.

See famous Russian writers buried here at 2 p.m. on Mondays and Thursdays.

He said he would speak to Sister Rita in the men's room.

Tom thought he saw a ghost on his way home from the cemetery.

He arrived to attend his son's wedding with Mr Brown.

We will not sell petrol to anyone in a glass container.

She told me she was going to have a baby in the middle of Oxford St.

Man gets 10 years in cello case.

Memo for staff with attachments (title of e-mail message)

In some cases phrases specifying a location present an ambiguity. Do they refer to a part of the body or to a more general location?

Where did you feel the pain?
In the kitchen.

Were you hurt in the melee?
No, in the stomach.

Where did she kiss you? Behind the ear?
No, behind the bike sheds.

In the next example the *wife* is in bed, but the phrase *with the doctor* presents a problem. Is it a further specification of the wife's location?

A: How's your wife?

B: She's in bed with the doctor.
A: She couldn't be too bad then.

The next example involves the scope of the in-phrase and a pun as well.

You mean he was shot in the woods?
No, I said he was shot in the lumbar region.

There can also be problems of scope where an adjective precedes a sequence of two nouns.

Henry is an old woman chaser.

The sequence *woman chaser* can be taken as a compound, though the two parts are written as separate words, and *old* can modify, or have scope over, the compound to give the reading 'Henry is a woman chaser who is old'. But *woman* and *chaser* can be taken as separate nouns with *old* modifying, or having scope over, just *woman* to give the reading, 'Henry chases old women'. Someone I know makes jokes by deliberately misgrouping. For instance, someone says, 'She's waiting over there in the park near the old female toilet' and he remarks, 'Oh, so they have toilets specially for old females.'

A similar problem of scope occurs with relative clauses when they follow an *of-* phrase.

Teachers of children who are married are entitled to an extra allowance.

Participial clauses

Consider the sentence *Flying over the plains we saw a herd of elephants*. The *-ing* form of the verb, that is, the present participle, has no subject. One deduces that the missing subject is the subject of the main verb *saw*. Now suppose we put the *flying-over-the-plains* clause at the end, to get *We saw a herd of elephants flying over* *the plains.* Compare this with *We saw a flock of geese flying over the plains.* We assume that it is 'we' who are flying over the plains, not the elephants, since elephants can't fly. There isn't any strict grammatical rule that enables us to work out who is flying, though there is a commonsense rule-of-thumb to the effect that one should not leave the participial clause without a readily identifiable subject. Here are some humorous examples that exploit this source of ambiguity. The first two examples are from actual news reports.

The accident broke her back and she also had internal injuries. After lying on her back for weeks, the doctor decided to operate.

More than 100 British MPs have assailed the Prince [Charles] after taking his two young sons hunting.

Driving across the plains, the zebras made a strange sight.

I saw a draught horse sitting in my car outside the station.

Co-ordination

Where nouns are joined by *and*, it is not always clear exactly what is being co-ordinated. In the first two examples it is not clear whether the adjective has scope over one noun or more. In the third example it is not clear, at least from the grammar, whether the *sumo wrestler* is being co-ordinated with the *woman* or the *baby*.

Lowest prices and service

Hirsute men and women

I saw a woman carrying a baby and a sumo wrestler.

The defendant was accompanied to court by a priest and his girlfriend.

In the next pair of examples the problem is to work out whether the last word is a noun or a verb. This then determines what it should be co-ordinated with. Of course, in written form, there is only one answer—*peas* is a noun and so is *fleas*—but you have to imagine them spoken.

He cuts up the onions and cries. Then he cuts up the beans and peas.

Prisoner escapes net and fleas.

The last example below involves co-ordination, but the real problem is with ellipsis. What noun do you fill in after 'second'?

Mr Johnson has three children and his wife Kerry is his second.

Missing subjects and objects

The abbreviated language of headlines, advertisements, particularly classified ads, recipes and instructions accompanying medicine provide ample scope for ambiguity caused by missing subjects and objects. In the first example it is a question of whether *flies* is the subject of the second sentence or whether the subject is missing.

Minister for the Environment delighted. Flies to wed.

In the next example, 'occupied' has no subject, and the reader is expected to make a reasonable assumption about what is occupied.

Cottage, 2 bedrooms, lounge, kitchen, bathroom, separate WC, occupied until end of month.

With recipes and instructions for taking medicine the object of the verb is frequently omitted on the grounds that it is obvious what the object is, for instance, *Shake before taking*. But it is not always obvious. A neighbour of mine was bottling fruit and came to the instruction *Boil bottle and cork*. She took *bottle* and *cork* to be objects of the verb *boil* and proceeded to boil them both. Here are some other examples where one might pause over the interpretation.

Rinse cups and stand in sink.

Rinse urn and stand upside down.

Wash before stewing.

Wash potatoes and peel.

Here's a different type of problem concerning an object. Does *wake up* take an object in the following or not?

Sometimes I wake up grumpy. Other times I let him sleep.

Pronouns and other problems of reference

As mentioned in Chapter 1 the majority of words refer consistently, usually to entities outside language. The noun *book* always refers to certain objects that have pages, the verb *swallow* always refers to the action of taking food or drink down the throat, and *orange* always refers to the colour of a familiar fruit. But there are also words that have variable reference, and the largest class of these words is the class of pronouns, words like *me*, *you*, *her* and *them*. *He*, *she* and *they* can refer to people in the vicinity or people previously mentioned. *It* can refer to all sorts of things or nothing at all as in *It is raining*. Some jokes are based on the fact that pronouns have variable reference and on the fact that one can sometimes select an unlikely candidate for the referent. Consider the advertisement that reads *Once people see our watches / They are sold*. What does *they* refer to? It could be the *watches*, but it could be *people*. The ambiguity is obvious and is designed to capture the attention of whoever reads the ad.

A well-known joke exploiting the ambiguity of pronouns goes like this: *If I told you you had a beautiful body, would you hold it against me?*, and there's the story about an announcement at the beginning of a mothers' club meeting that read *For those who have children and don't know it, there's a changing room at the end of the corridor.*

One time when I was teaching an English class, the French expression *je ne sais quoi* came up in the material we were reading. I asked the class what it meant and one student offered a not-very-clear version of the meaning, so I said, 'Suppose you had the sentence "She had a certain *je ne sais quoi* about her".' Another student gave the paraphrase, 'She had something that you couldn't put your finger on.' The class was not slow to pick up the unintended referent of the pronoun *something*!

In the next example *that* is the problem.

Doctor: How are you feeling today?
Patient: My breathing still troubles me.
Doctor: Mm! We must put a stop to that.

And in the next two you need to think about *they* and *them*.

Arts 2004 will feature an exhibition of over 1200 paintings by young artists. They were all executed since Arts 2002.

Keep all poisons in the bathroom cupboard. If there are children in the house, lock them up.

In the next example *they* is again the problem, but there is also an ambiguity in *cast off clothing*.

The ladies have cast off clothing. They can be seen in the church hall after 1.00 p.m.

And finally the pronoun *it*, which probably offers more scope for ambiguity than any other.

Mother, I've just found out that my fiancé has a wooden leg. Do you think I should break it off?

A woman walked into a pharmacy and spoke to the pharmacist.
She asked, 'Do you have Viagra?'
'Yes,' he replied.
She asked, 'Does it work?'
'Yes,' he answered.
'Can you get it over the counter?' she asked.
'I can if I take two,' he answered.

In the next example the noun *place* is rather like a pronoun in that one needs to look back (or 'hear back') to see what it refers to. It could be the *cottage* or the *pool*. The same problem arises with the pronoun *it*. Under one interpretation, it sounds as if one might be involved in imbibing excessive amounts of liquid.

Charming cottage, three bedrooms. Breathtaking mountain views. Heated pool. The perfect place to relax and drink it all in.

Variations on the next joke have been circulating for some time. When I first heard it, it included a reference to George Bush the elder, but it can now be taken to refer to George Bush the younger. The joke exploits the ambiguity of the pronoun 'one', and it also illustrates a type of joke in which the listener or reader is led down the garden path. It is in the form of a riddle.

What is the subject of the following statements?
George Bush has a short one.
Arnold Schwarzenegger has a big one.
The Pope has one, but he doesn't use it.
Cher doesn't have one at all.

What is it?
A second name.

In the next example the problem is whether *yourself* should be taken as a reflexive pronoun as in 'He cleans himself' or intensive as in 'He himself cleans'.

Tired of cleaning yourself? Let our trained staff do it for you.

Similar to the above are cases where nouns are used in a context where they could be referring to one person or a class of persons. In the first example below 'a man' could, in theory, refer to one particular man or to a series of different men.

A: There's a report in the paper here that in New York a man is mugged every three hours.
B: But after the first mugging he would have nothing left.

Father: I think it is time you took a wife.
Son: Whose wife should I take?

Nouns such as *king*, *queen*, *mayor* and *minister* can refer to anyone holding the office designated by the term. When Pope Paul VI died in 1978, a new pope, John Paul I, was elected. He died a month later. One tabloid ran the headline *Pope dies again*.

The next example revolves around the interpretation of 'six miles'. Suppose your doctor told you to walk six miles every day. I imagine you would walk three miles from your home and three miles back, but this would not be specified in the doctor's instruction.

My father read about the importance of keeping fit if you want to live long, so when he reached 65 and retired, he began to walk six miles each day and we haven't seen him since.

The next joke is easy to get, but you might take a little more time to see where the ambiguity lies. The word *so* is the culprit. Try an innocuous example such as *John eats potatoes and so does Fred*. What does Fred do? He eats potatoes. OK? Now, in the next example, what do half the men in the country do?

Bill sleeps with his wife seven nights a week. Nothing remarkable about that, so do half the men in this country.

There can also be ambiguity with expressions of quantity such as *all* or *some* or numerals such as *two*, where they are used without any specification of what is being quantified.

Doctor (on home visit to husband): I suppose you're giving him all he wants.
Wife: Oh, doctor, he's been far too sick for anything like that.

7
Jokes

Besides puns and other witticisms that can be slipped into the conversation, usually based on something that happens to come up in the context, there are what we might call formal jokes. To signal that he or she is about to tell a joke, the teller might say, 'I heard this really good joke' or might ask, 'Did you hear the one about ...?' They might use one of a number of question formulas which we are meant to recognize as setting up punchlines. These include 'What do you get if you cross x with y?' or 'How many so-and-so's does it take to change a light bulb?' What follows is a collection of jokes classified into a number of standard types or formats. Some of these jokes are normally oral, some are pretty much peculiar to the printed mode, and a few could appear in either mode. A few are like the following and depend on spelling.

Did you know that was a wildebeest?
Yes, I gnu.

When people think about jokes, they are most likely to think of the story-type joke or anecdote-type joke, so these are illustrated first. The other types are presented in alphabetic order.

Stories

The most common 'story' joke contains three parts, all parallel, with the punchline in the third part. The interview with the IRA bomber in Chapter 1 was in that format. Another type has only two parts and concerns someone receiving good news and bad news.

> A man goes into hospital to have a leg amputated. When he wakes up after the operation, the doctor says, 'I've got some good news and some bad news. Which do you want to hear first?'
> 'The bad news,' says the patient.
> 'Well, the bad news is that we've taken the wrong leg off.'
> 'Oh, no!' says the patient. 'What's the good news?'
> 'The other leg turned out to be all right!'

Here are a few more story-type jokes, some short and some long.

> The British Prime Minister, Tony Blair, was visiting the Middle East. One day he went for a walk in the desert and stumbled upon a dusty old lamp. He picked it up and rubbed it, and suddenly a genie appeared, just as in those stories of Aladdin and co. Tony asked the genie if he could have three wishes.
> 'No,' said the genie, 'those days are gone. Nowadays you get just one wish. What would you like?'
> Tony said, 'I want to be able to broker a lasting peace in the Middle East. See this map? I want to stop the fighting between Jews and Arabs once and for all.'
> The genie looked at the map of the Middle East and shook his head, 'I don't think I can do that. These people have been at war for years, and there are really bitter differences between them. I'm a pretty good genie, but I'm not that good. Make another wish.'

Tony thought for a minute and said, 'I've lost a lot of support. The Iraq war hasn't turned out too well. Even my Labour Party supporters are falling off. I want you to make me popular again with all the people of Britain.'

The genie pursed up his lips, sucked in his breath and said, 'Let's have a look at that map again.'

A language teacher was explaining to her class that French nouns, unlike their English counterparts, are grammatically designated as masculine or feminine. 'Window', for instance, is *la fenêtre*, feminine, and 'pencil' is *le crayon*, masculine.

One student put up his hand and asked, 'What gender is a computer?'

The teacher didn't know and so she divided the class by gender and asked them to decide whether a computer should be masculine or feminine. Each group was asked to give four reasons for its recommendation.

The female students concluded that computers should be referred to in the masculine gender because:

- In order to get their attention, you have to turn them on.
- They have a lot of data but are still clueless.
- They are supposed to help you solve your problems, but half the time they ARE the problem.
- As soon as you commit to one, you realize that, if you had waited a little longer, you could have had a better model.

The male students, on the other hand, decided that computers should definitely be referred to in the feminine gender because:

- No one but their creator understands their internal logic.
- The native language they use to communicate with other computers is incomprehensible to everyone else.
- Even your smallest mistakes are stored in long-term memory for later retrieval.

• As soon as you make a commitment to one, you find
  yourself spending half your pay on accessories for it.

A woman wants a dog, so she buys a Schnauzer. After a
while, she discovers that it is developing an unsightly
growth of hair around the ears, so she goes to the chemist
to get some depilatory cream. The chemist recommends a
particular brand, which he says is excellent. 'But', he says,
'it is very abrasive. If you are using it on your legs, don't
leave it on for more than half an hour. If you are using it
under your arms, fifteen minutes. And if you are using it
on your face, just five minutes.' 'But it is for my Schnauzer,' the woman replies. 'In that case,' says the chemist,
'don't ride a bicycle for at least a week.'

Three nuns die in an accident and find themselves in a
queue in front of the Pearly Gates. Eventually they get to
St Peter. He checks their records on his computer and con-
gratulates them on their lives of virtue. 'However,' he says,
'entry to Heaven is no longer as straightforward as it once
was. I'm under instructions to tighten up a bit. If you
want to go straight inside, you each need to answer a ques-
tion on the Bible correctly. Otherwise you must remain
for a period in a detention centre (formerly Purgatory).'
St Peter says to the first nun, 'I've got an easy one for you.
Who was the first man on Earth?'
'Adam,' says the first nun.
'Right,' says Peter. 'Go through.'
To the second nun he says, 'I've got another easy one for
you. Who was the first woman on earth?'
'Eve,' says the second nun.
'Very good,' says Peter. 'Go through and join your friend.'
St Peter then looks at the third nun and at his computer
screen and he frowns. 'Mm, although you've been a pretty
good nun, there were a few little things like the mission
money that disappeared just before the Derby one year. I

think you need a more difficult question. What were the very first words Eve uttered when she first saw Adam?' The third nun ponders for a while and she thinks she'll have to give up. She looks at Peter hoping for some help and says, 'That's a hard one.' 'Good girl,' says Peter. 'You're in. Go and join your friends.'

Books

There are two kinds of written joke featuring books: funny titles and suggestions for what would make a very, very short book.

Book titles

The Russian Counter-tenor by Ivor Nackeroff

The Men's Room by I. P. Standing

Praying Mantras by Neil Down

The Sadistic Schoolmaster by Ben Dover

Coping with Bad Weather by Ivor Macintosh

Know Your Limitations by Eamonn Low

Mining Profits by Nick L. Orr

Holidaying in Florida by Sonny Daye

Shortest books

America's Most Popular Lawyers

Bill Clinton's *Guide to Family Values*

Dan Quayle's *Guide to Clear Thinking* (with a foreword by George W. Bush)

Maggie Thatcher's *Best Jokes*

Mike Tyson's Guide to Dating Etiquette

The Amish Phone Directory

The Al Qaeda Pension Plan

Walking Holidays in Antarctica

Blonde jokes

The 'blonde' in this genre is always dumb and not averse to a bit of sex with whomever.

Why does a blonde keep a coathanger on the back seat of her car?
In case she locks her keys in the car.

What does a blonde say when she finds she's pregnant?
Is it mine?

How does a blonde turn on the light after sex?
She opens the car door!

Why was the blonde so pleased when she finished the jigsaw puzzle in six months?
Because it said on the box 'Three to five years'.

Cannibal jokes

Europeans encountered cannibals when they embarked on colonial expansion and cannibals exerted a curious fascination. Something of the European attitude can be seen in the following passage from the beginning of Part II of Evelyn Waugh's comic novel *Scoop*. Ishmaelia is a mythical north-eastern African state.

Various courageous Europeans, in the seventies of the last [nineteenth] century, came to Ishmaelia, or near it, fur-

nished with suitable equipment of cuckoo clocks, phonographs, opera hats, draft treaties and flags of the nations they had been obliged to leave. They came as missionaries, ambassadors, tradesmen, prospectors, natural scientists. None returned. They were eaten, every one of them; some raw, others stewed and seasoned—according to local usage and the calendar (for the better sort of Ishmaelites have been Christian for many centuries and will not publicly eat human flesh, uncooked, in Lent, without special and costly dispensation from their bishop).

Waugh's humour derives from the matter-of-fact treatment of something Europeans find revolting. Cannibal jokes derive their humour in a similar way.

Young cannibal: What are we having for dinner?
Mother cannibal: The colonial administrator.
Young cannibal: I hate his guts!
Mother cannibal: Well, just leave them and eat up your vegetables.

Father cannibal: What are we having for dinner tonight?
Mother cannibal: Fried spinster.
Father cannibal: Oh, no. Not leftovers again.

Why did the cannibal spit out the clown?
Because he tasted funny.

What did the cannibal say when he found the white hunter asleep?
'Ah, breakfast in bed.'

What did the cannibal detective have for dinner?
Grilled suspect.

Father cannibal: I smell someone burning.

Mother cannibal: I'm worried about my little boy. He's got nausea, and he can't keep anyone down.

Father cannibal: Am I late for dinner?

Mother cannibal: Yes, everybody's eaten.

Dumb jokes

We've probably all done something which in retrospect seems completely stupid, like asking someone how long they've had their birthmark. A priest once told me that as Christmas approaches each year he gets the odd caller ringing up to ask, 'What time is Midnight Mass?' And somewhere I saw recently an instruction to address envelopes before posting. Dumb jokes depict people as more stupid than one could possibly imagine. They are often directed against a particular nationality, but in the spirit of political correctness I have disguised the ethnicity of the butt in the first example below. As a class they overlap with blonde jokes, but, as the examples above show, blonde jokes can involve promiscuity as well as dumbness.

Mrs O'Toole (a Patagonian woman) hears a knock at the door. When she opens it, there's a policeman holding a severed head. 'I'm sorry to trouble you, ma'am, but there's been a terrible accident and this man has been decapitated and we wondered if it was Mr O'Toole.' 'Oh, no,' says Mrs O'Toole. 'My husband's a much taller man.'

One morning Fred gets a job in a sawmill. After he has been there for an hour or so, he calls out, 'Damn! I've lost a finger.' The foreman is quite concerned since the company is very anxious about its safety record. 'How did that happen?' he asks. 'I just touched this big spinning thing. Damn. There goes another one.'

Why did the British couple stop after three kids?
Because they read that every fourth child in the world is
Chinese.

A: What's Mick's other name?
B: Mick who?

Dumb jokes are also directed against individuals: politicians,
film stars, pop stars and sports stars. In the example below, football star David Beckham and his wife, Posh Spice, of Spice Girls
fame, are featured.

**Posh and Becks are sitting in front of the television watch-
ing the six o'clock news. The main story is about a man
threatening to jump off a bridge onto a busy road below
and kill himself.
Posh turns to Becks and says, 'David, I bet you £5000
that he jumps!'
Beckham replies, '£5000? Done! I bet you that he doesn't.'
So they shake hands on the bet and continue watching.
Sure enough, the man jumps and hits the road below with
a sickening thud and splatters. Beckham takes £5000 out
of his back pocket and hands it to Posh, but she refuses. 'I
can't take your money, David,' she says. 'The truth is, I
was cheating. I saw the five o'clock news, so I knew he
was going to jump.'
'I saw the five o'clock news too,' says David, 'but I just
didn't think he would do it again.'**

Definitions

Funny definitions abound. Some of the following appeared among
the winning entries of the *Washington Post* contest in which en-
trants are asked to supply alternative meanings for words. Most
are in general circulation in joke collections. The first batch below deals with the human body and its problems.

adenoid: irritated by commercials on TV

aperitif: French dentures

Caesarian section: the downtown area of Rome

flabbergasted: aghast at how much weight you've put on

humerus: funny bone

impotence: no hard feelings

innuendo: Italian suppository

outpatient: an unconscious person

penicillin: for the man who has everything

rectitude: the solemn demeanour of a proctologist

shin: a device for finding furniture in the dark

willy-nilly: impotent

And now a few miscellaneous definitions:

A fine: a tax for doing wrong. A tax: a fine for doing well.

chinchilla: aftershave

coffee: person coughed upon

counter-culture: retail

dilate: to live a long time

dumb waiter: one who asks if the kids would care to order dessert

feedback: the result of giving babies something they don't like

homophone: gay speech

laughing-stock: cattle with a sense of humour

show-off: a child more talented than one's own

truculent: lorry you borrowed

Generalizations and exhortations

The e-mail of the species is more deadly than the mail.

Egotists don't talk about other people.

Women like silent men; they think they're listening.

Atheism is a non-prophet organization.

Pride is what we have. Vanity is what others have.

Familiarity breeds children.

Better late than pregnant.

Learn from your parents' mistakes—use birth control.

Remember the poor—it costs nothing.

Graffiti

Graffiti have a long history. While archaeologists have found graffiti in the ruins of ancient cities, they are extraordinarily common at the present time. They range from signatures ('tags'), names and rude words through brief texts to various forms of art. Traditionally they are found in toilets, waiting rooms and telephone boxes, as well as on non-residential walls, but recently they have spread to garden walls, sides of houses and the like.

Some graffiti are political. One of the first examples of political graffiti I can remember seeing was in the 1960s. It read *Worker, your tiny wage is frozen*, playing on *Your tiny hand is frozen*, the famous aria from Puccini's *La Bohème*. A more up-to-date (well, 1980s) example was *Keep the gay whales in the ground*. This was a widely distributed pseudo-slogan, which managed to package a number of contemporary protests into one.

Graffiti are cheap and available to anyone with a paintbrush or a spray can. Where there is censorship, opponents of the regime often resort to graffiti to get their message across, and as a means of communication graffiti can be quite effective. Even in the tolerant regimes of the West one can learn a lot about the mood of the underclass from the themes found in graffiti. Unfortunately, one also finds a lot of abuse directed towards ethnic minorities and gays.

Here we are concerned with those texts that carry a witty or humorous message. Recently I saw among a large collection of graffiti the following brief poem:

When I walk along this street
By God I wish I could graffite!

There's no doubt that graffiti can be entertaining, though they do not represent a type of humour. Any short joke or witty remark can be sprayed on a wall, and general statements like those given above in the section on 'Generalizations and exhortations' frequently appear on walls. But there is one type that is peculiar to graffiti and that is variations on something like *Arsenal rules OK*? These originated as aggressive territorial claims by gangs of youths and then as a kind of territorial claim by supporters of football teams. Here is an example of the kind of variation you get.

Muhammad Ali rules KO?
The queen rules UK.
Dyslexia lures KO

Another territorial type of graffiti reads 'No so-and-so here' and sets out to make those of another religion, race or sexual preference unwelcome. Here is an example from Northern Ireland and a riposte.

No pope here
Lucky pope

Religious messages also find themselves on walls from time to time. The following example of statement and addendum occurs widely, with variations as to the financial institution.

Jesus saves
With the Credit Union

As mentioned in Chapter 1, it is common to find dialogue in graffiti, but there is also the possibility that one person uses the first part as a feed line and adds the punchline him- or herself.

As with other jokes, graffiti humour circulates. Some examples quoted on the internet from a particular location can be found at a variety of other locations, as with the following example.

A woman's rule of thumb: if it has tyres or testicles, you're going to have trouble with it.

And finally a nice example of a piece of wit that could hardly be presented successfully in any other medium. It is a statement-and-rejoinder type, but probably both from the same hand. After all, would anyone bother to inscribe just the feed line?

God is dead.
Nietzsche

Nietzsche is dead.
God

Headlines

Some headlines were presented in Chapter 3, which hinged on different structural interpretations of a sequence of words, but there are other types of humorous headline. Headlines have to be brief, because words must fit a space. This sometimes means compromising on clarity of meaning.

Schoolboy suspended by head
Blind bishop appointed to see
Council accused of digging own grave
Toilets held up by red tape
March planned for April
Patient at death's door—doctors pull him through
Queen Mary having bottom scraped
Patients waiting for major surgery cut in half
Strike at knitting mill. Women's skirts held up
US treads softly on landmines

How many x's does it take to change a light bulb?

This is a strange category. You might wonder how the question 'How many so-and-so's does it take to change a light bulb?' came to be the basis for a series of jokes. Part of the reason for the proliferation of the type is that you can create a joke about any race, nationality, trade, profession, political party, or other identifiable interest group, with the punchline being specific to the perceived characteristics of that group.

How many jugglers does it take to change a light bulb?
Only one but it takes at least three light bulbs.

How many magicians does it take to change a light bulb?
Depends on what you want to change it into.

How many straight guys does it take to change a light bulb in San Francisco?
Both of them.

How many chiropractors does it take to change a light
bulb?
Only one, but it will take twenty visits.

How many telemarketers does it take to change a light
bulb?
Only one, but he has to do it while you're eating.

How many Jewish mothers does it take to change a light
bulb?
None. Don't mind me. I'll just sit here in the dark.

Knock knock!

Knock-knock jokes are usually childish. They are initiated by
one person approaching another and saying, 'Knock knock!' The
addressee is supposed to respond, 'Who's there?' and the joke is
on.

Knock knock!
Who's there?
Lettuce.
Lettuce who?
Let us in.

Knock knock!
Who's there?
Isabel.
Isabel who?
Is a bell necessary on a bicycle?

Oxymora and other self-contradictions

The **oxymoron** is a traditional rhetorical device in which the
modifier in a construction appears to contradict the modified. In
a typical example an adjective appears to contradict a noun, as in

democratic tyrant. Other common examples are *deafening silence*, *hasten slowly*, *sweet sorrow* and *timeless moment*. In each case one has to try and resolve the anomaly between the adjective and the noun. Instances such as *plastic glasses, work party* and *tight slacks* are sometimes given as examples, but in these cases the meaning of the noun has been extended so that the combination in fact makes perfect sense, and similarly with phrases such as *pretty ugly* and *awfully decent* where the modifier has lost its literal meaning in these contexts. I've seen the sentence *Thank God I'm an atheist* (attributed to various people) given as an example of an oxymoron, and there is a certain irony in it, to be sure, but the expression *Thank God* has become so conventionalized as to have little religious connotation. Another example of this kind of thing would be a *well-ordered disorderly house*, which appears to contain a contradiction, but doesn't, because *disorderly house* is a euphemism for 'brothel'. I often think of oxymora when I'm trying to remove indurated food from the non-stick frying-pan, but the truth is that non-stick products don't remain non-stick forever. I came across an advertisement for a private school that said students were required to do some voluntary work, but I suppose that meant they had to do some kind of unpaid work, of the type normally done by volunteers. I must confess I don't know what to think of the application form for travel insurance that asked, 'Have you ever suffered from a terminal illness?' I suppose I can be generous and interpret this to mean something like 'Have you ever had a life-threatening condition, something that would have been terminal if measures hadn't been taken?' (no pun intended with 'measures').

But even at my most generous I'm a-mused and be-mused by the magazine that promised to publish a 'complete extract' from a novel. What would an incomplete extract look like? I wonder what happened to the footballer who claimed he was kneed with an elbow. I am suspicious of the store that offers *exclusive swimwear: something for everyone*, and I am critical of the auctioneers who describe item 31 in their catalogue as 'unique' and then put *ditto* for item 32.

In current usage the term **oxymoron** is most often used for
two-word phrases where the choice of modifier (usually adjective) with a particular head (usually noun) is incongruous or can
be taken in an ironical or satirical way. Sometimes the irony is
only apparent from the appearance of a phrase in a list of
oxymora. For instance, one does not usually find anything incongruous about the term *political science*, but when it is given in a
list of oxymora, one can see the irony.

A little pregnant	Childproof
Airline food	Computer security
Almost exactly	Definite maybe
Business ethics	Essential luxury
Exact estimate	Minor disaster
Extinct life	Non-working mother
Genuine imitation	Resident alien
Government efficiency	Sure bet
Government organization	Taped live
Honest politician	Temporary tax increase
Instant classic	Working vacation
Military intelligence	

I came across the following sentences given as examples of
oxymora, but perhaps they just illustrate excessive use of certain
metaphorical expressions.

I saw her listening out of the corner of her eye.

This is virgin territory pregnant with possibilities.

Better examples are the following from the Hollywood producer
Sam Goldwyn (the 'G' of MGM).

If you fall and break your legs, don't come running to me.

A verbal contract isn't worth the paper it's written on.

Sam Goldwyn is often quoted as a source of some linguistic oddity or another. One of the most quoted sayings attributed to him is *Include me out*, which has claims to being an oxymoron. Sometimes people make statements that are contradicted by the very act of saying them, as with *I'm not going to say, 'I told you so.'* This kind of thing is exploited in jokes where a prohibition incorporates an example of the error.

Never generalize.

Don't be racist. Wogs are easily offended.

Prepositions are not words to end sentences with.

The last of these is a variant of a well-known (but stupid) rule of grammar: 'Don't end a sentence with a preposition.' In the film *Pillow Talk* there is a clever play on this rule where Doris Day (the virgin) rebukes Rock Hudson (the wolf) with the words 'There are some men who don't end every sentence with a proposition.' Here is another type of joke that exploits the internal contradiction or paradox.

Economists have forecast ten out of the last six recessions.

Van Eyck painted 300 pictures. Of these 350 have been found so far and more are turning up each year.

When I was young, I would have given my right hand to be ambidextrous.

People can have it [the Model T Ford] in any colour, as long as it's black.

Henry Ford

Questions

This is a large miscellaneous class. All that they have in common is that they are introduced by a question in a context where the question is irrelevant and you therefore know that you are being offered a joke.

Why do Greeks have bigger balls than Italians?
Because they sell more tickets.

Why are there so many Smiths in the phone book?
They all have phones.

Why is Clinton so interested in events in the Middle East?
He thinks the Gaza Strip is a topless bar.

Why is a wedding anniversary like a toilet seat?
Men miss both.

What did the woman do who didn't like her baby?
She went to the baby changing room.

What does a masochist do when he gets home after a hard day at the office?
He likes to slip into something uncomfortable.

What is the difference between a pregnant woman and a light bulb?
You can unscrew a light bulb.

What's the definition of a will?
It's a dead give-away.

Signs

Most of these signs are reported as genuine and the originals were probably posted seriously. However, some signs are deliberately funny. There is a hotel in the USA called *Big Dick's Halfway Inn* and somewhere in the same country there is a golf-course with a sign that goes, *Persons collecting golf balls will be prosecuted and have their balls removed.* In Darwin there is *Burke's Brassiere*, presumably a deliberate misspelling.

In a restaurant: *If you don't like our waiters, you should see the manager.*

In an optometrist's office: *If you don't see what you want, we can help you.*

In a travel agent's window: *Go away!*

In a vet's waiting room: *Sit!*

In a laundromat: *Remove all clothing before leaving.*

On a highway: *When this sign is under water, this road is impassable.*

At a pedestrian crossing: *Elderly cross here.*

Outside a school: *No trespassing without permission.*

Outside antique shop: *Remains to be seen.*

On divorce lawyer's wall: *Satisfaction guaranteed or your honey back.*

Outside clinic: *Hours 9.00–5.00. Emergencies only after hours.*

Outside maternity ward: *No children allowed.*

At a military base: *Restricted to unauthorized personnel.*

Outside the monkey house at the zoo: *Do not feed the monkeys. Give peanuts to the keepers.*

Outside pharmacist's shop: *We dispense with accuracy.*

Outside second-hand shop: *We buy junk and sell antiques.*

Outside hospital: *Dogs operate in this area.*

Outside kindergarten: *Infant teacher required.*

Stickers

It is common nowadays for jokes to appear on the bumpers or rear windows of cars or on the back of vans and trucks. Here are some that relate to driving a car, but some of the other joke categories listed in this chapter sometimes appear on cars.

Honk if you love peace and quiet.

Horn broken. Watch for finger.

Mafia staff car. Hands off.

No radio—already stolen.

My other car is a Merc.

The following are also frequently seen as bumper stickers, well, at least those relating to trades. We never get to find out what 'it' is.

Assassins do it from behind.

Carpenters do it with their tools.

Electricians do it with power.

Fisherman do it with their rods.

Mechanics do it with their wenches.

Tom Swifties

Tom Swift and his son were the heroes of a series of adventure books for boys. Tom Swift Senior was featured in a series of books from 1910 to 1941 and Tom Swift Junior in a series that ran from 1954 to 1971. Young Tom hardly ever spoke without the author adding an adverb so we had 'Tom said slowly' or 'Tom said jokingly'. These adverbs were so plentiful that they gave rise to a type of joke known as a **Tom Swiftie**, in which the adverb is chosen to relate to the content of what is said or to pun on part of what is said.

'And she has whiskers,' said Sue cattily.

'I need a pencil sharpener,' said Tom bluntly.

'That's a vicious circle,' said Tom roundly.

'I wouldn't marry Hamlet,' she said disdainfully.

'I'd certainly appreciate a triple by-pass', he said wholeheartedly.

'Drop your guns. I've got you covered,' she said disarmingly.

'I want you to neutralize the enemy base,' said the colonel acidly.

'It'll cost you 50 quid, sweetie,' she said tartly.

'I want to marry you,' she said engagingly.

Wellerisms

Wellerisms are named after Sam Weller in Dickens's *The Post-humous Papers of the Pickwick Club*, better known as *The Pickwick Papers*. These expressions consist of a phrase in the form 'as X said to Y', which Sam adds to some of his utterances. A comparison of the *as*-statement and the utterance to which it is appended usually involves some kind of play on words. The following example is from the beginning of Chapter XXXVII. Sam has just received a letter addressed to him.

'Very odd that,' said Sam. 'I'm afeerd there must be
somethin' the matter, for I don't recollect any gen'l'm'n in
my circle of acquaintances as is capable o' writin' one.'
'Perhaps something uncommon has taken place,' observed
Mrs Craddock.
'It must be somethin' wery uncommon indeed as could
perduce a letter out o' any friend o' mine,' replied Sam,
shaking his head dubiously, 'nothing less than a nat'ral
conwulsion as the young gen'l'm'n observed ven he vos
took with fits.'

Here are some other examples of Wellerisms:

'I'll meet you at the corner,' as one wall said to the other.

'Guess again,' as the poultry farmer said to the chicken
sexer.

'Out with it,' as the mother said to the child who had
swallowed the sixpence.

'I was OK at the rehearsal this morning,' as the blue movie
stud said to the director.

'May I leave the table?' as the white ant asked his parents.

What do you get if you cross *x* with *y*?

This is a popular type of joke and is introduced with the question
'What do you get if you cross so-and-so with so-and-so?'

**What do you get if you cross Big Ben with the Leaning
Tower of Pisa?**
The time AND the inclination.

**What do you get if you cross Peter Pan with a travel-
sickness pill?**

A boy who'll never throw up.

What do you get if you cross a computer and one million mosquitoes?
A gigabyte.

What is the difference between *x* and *y*?

Another popular type of joke is recognizable from the question *What is the difference between x and y?* Note the pithy replies, especially for the last two examples.

> What's the difference between ignorance and apathy?
> I don't know and I don't care.

> What's the difference between herpes and true love?
> Herpes lasts forever.

> What's the difference between a sensitive new-age guy and a male chauvinist?
> Two beers.

> What's the difference between Niagara and Viagra?
> Niagara Falls.

All the questions given above expect an answer, at least nominally, in fact they expect that the addressee will not be able to answer. There are also observations in question form such as, 'How come the only people who are capable of running the country are either driving taxis or cutting hair?' There are also a few wry one-line jokes in question form such as *Before they invented drawing boards, what did they go back to?* These are normally written rather than spoken.

8

Wit

The terms 'humour' and 'wit' overlap. We can make a distinction, though the difference is certainly not clear-cut. Wit is cleverness with words, usually humorous, but not always. The author is demonstrating his or her verbal prowess. We are meant to admire the ingenuity, perhaps we will smile, perhaps even laugh, but if we do, that is a bonus. Since the term 'wit' is generally reserved for the clever end of the humour spectrum, the following with their clever transpositions would qualify.

A hangover is the wrath of grapes.

Time's fun when you're having flies.

Kermit the Frog

What is the difference between a warder and a jeweller?
One watches cells and the other sells watches.

What is the difference between a ball and a prince?
One is thrown in the air and the other is heir to the throne.

The following examples on a Cartesian theme would also qualify. There is a quotation from Descartes that every educated person is expected to know, and we are also expected to know that the name of this famous thinker is pronounced 'day cart'. The quote is *Cogito ergo sum*, which is Latin for 'I think, therefore I am'. Now someone turns it around and it comes out as *Sum ergo cogito*, 'I am, therefore I think'. Now this is clever for a start, but then some wag adds, 'Isn't that putting Des-cartes before de-horse?' Now, keeping the famous quote in mind, consider the following.

Descartes walks into a restaurant and sits down ready to order. A waiter comes up to him and asks, 'Would you like a menu?' Descartes replies, 'I think not,' and he disappears!

An anonymous graffitist inscribed a variant *Coitus ergo sum*. You can't argue with that. Without *coitus*, we wouldn't exist. A number of people have tried their hand at variations on the original quote including the woman who wrote *I think, therefore I am single*.

Certain writers are noted for their wit, including Oscar Wilde, who produced

Work is the curse of the drinking classes.

This is clever in that it swaps two words in the phrasing of what was a common sentiment. One difference between the Wilde quotation and the first four examples above is that Wilde's makes a statement about society, whereas the other two offer no worthwhile substance. People who are regarded as witty are those who produce cleverly phrased opinions or sentiments. You could repeat the Wilde quote at a suitable point in a conversation or talk, but the other examples can only be repeated as jokes. This is in line with Pope's notion that true wit is the clever expression of a widely held observation or opinion, though presumably originality is not to be excluded.

**True wit is Nature to advantage dressed,
What oft was thought but ne'er so well expressed.**

Despite what the dictionary might say in trying to define 'wit', it is clear from a survey of usage that many reserve the term for something that employs ingenuity to express worthwhile, including serious, content. What follows is a small sample of what qualifies as wit either through cleverly phrased substance or from the demands it makes on the audience, as with the Descartes-in-the-restaurant example above.

I was once at a garden party in Australia where one of the guests had a four-year-old son called Tarquin. (Now why on earth someone would call their kid after the man who raped Lucrece I don't know, but that's what the poor kid was called.) Anyway, this child appeared at the party in a striking pair of multi-coloured pants. One of the guests referred to them as 'Tarquin's ravishing strides', very clever if you live in a part of the English-speaking world where 'strides' is a synonym for 'pants' or 'trousers' and if you remember Macbeth's words as he sets off to murder Duncan (Act II, scene i),

... and wither'd murder,
Alarum'd by his sentinel, the wolf,
Whose howl's his watch, thus with his stealthy pace,
With Tarquin's ravishing strides, towards his design
Moves like a ghost.

While this witticism depends on a literary allusion, the following clever joke requires a bit of thought before you realize the insulting impact of the man's reply. It is to be found in Freud but dates back to classical times.

A king was travelling through his kingdom when he noticed a man who bore a striking resemblance to himself. 'Was your mother ever in service at the palace?' he asked. 'No,' replied the man, 'but my father was.'

I don't know if the following anecdote is authentic, but Sir Winston Churchill was a witty man, and one can easily imagine him having come up with this particular piece of repartee.

Lady Astor: Had I been your wife, I would've poisoned your coffee.
Churchill: Had I been your husband, I would've drunk it.

As mentioned in the previous chapter, there is a silly old rule of prescriptive grammar that says you shouldn't end a sentence with a preposition. When someone rebuked Churchill for breaking the rule, he replied, 'That is the sort of English up with which I shall not put.'

Wit can be quite serious, though it must still display some verbal ingenuity. Some commentators on wit have seen it in negative terms, emphasizing its power to wound. Lord Chesterfield wrote that 'people fear it, and few love it unless in themselves.' Marya Mannes picked out the ability of wit to wound those one might consider good subjects for wounding, 'Wit has a deadly aim and it is possible to prick a large pretence with a small pin.' Some political cartoons use wit to make a serious point. In 1842 General Napier led British troops to victory over the Sindhis and brought the province of Sind under British control. The British invasion was of more than dubious morality and *Punch* published a cartoon showing Napier striding through the dead with the caption *Peccavi—I have sinned* (*peccavi* is Latin for 'I have sinned'). This is a very clever piece of language play, but not the sort of thing to make you laugh.

Gandhi was not a man noted for his humour, but he was once asked, 'What do you think of British civilization?' He replied, 'I think it would be a very good idea.' This is clever in that it undermines the assumption inherent in the question, namely, that British civilization exists.

Some writers specialize in wit. Oscar Wilde was undoubtedly a great example. On learning of the high cost of an operation he remarked, 'I suppose that I shall have to die beyond my means.' His works are full of the idle rich upper classes who delight in making smart and cynical observations. Lord Henry Wotton in *The Picture of Dorian Gray*, for instance, says, 'The only way to get rid of a temptation is to yield to it.' In *Lady Windermere's Fan* Lord Augustus Lorton tells us, 'I prefer women with a past. They're always so damned amusing to talk to', and the Duchess of Berwick says, 'Men become old, but they never become good.'

Much drama depends on unfaithfulness and Wilde's plays are full of cynicism about romance and marriage. Algernon in *The Importance of Being Earnest* provides a number of examples.

You don't seem to realise, that in married life three is company and two is none.

Divorces are made in Heaven.

If we compare the last remark with the next, we see something of the way Wilde's wit often involves taking an idiom or cliché and twisting it.

The amount of women in London who flirt with their own husbands is perfectly scandalous. It looks so bad. It is simply washing one's clean linen in public.

Some of his wit is trivial and merely involves ingenious wording, but some examples are aimed at making insightful observations. In the following exchange Wilde, through Algernon, gets to the heart of the latter kind of wit: clever phrasing and enough truth to seem plausible.

Algernon: All women become like their mothers. That is their tragedy. No man does. That's his.
Jack: Is that clever?
Algernon: It is perfectly phrased! And quite as true as any observation in civilised life should be.

Fifty-odd years after Wilde, Dorothy Parker demanded content as well as expression, 'Wit has truth in it, wisecracking is simply callisthenics with words.'

Until the advent of feminism it was the norm for women to be reticent about their age and, if a figure was revealed by a mature woman, there was often the suspicion that there had been some subtraction. Women's age is the subject of a number of Wilde's clever lines. In *A Woman of No Importance*, Lord Illingworth, on hearing that an American lady has revealed 'in quite a loud voice' that she is only eighteen, remarks,

One should never trust a woman who tells one her real age. A woman who would tell one that, would tell one anything.

And in *The Importance of Being Earnest*, Lady Bracknell observes,

Thirty-five is a very attractive age. London society is full of women of the very highest birth who have, of their own free choice, remained thirty-five for years.

Wilde also remarked that 'We have really everything in common with America nowadays except, of course, language.' The English like to think the Americans speak a foreign tongue, and that they alone preserve the true language. George Bernard Shaw once said that 'England and America are two countries separated by a common language.' Alan Jay Lerner, an American, puts a similar sentiment into the mouth of Professor Henry Higgins, who complains in the opening number of *My Fair Lady* about misuse of the English language and says 'In America they haven't used it for years.'

Another witty contemporary of Wilde was W. S. Gilbert (of Gilbert and Sullivan fame). He was once asked by a woman, 'Is Bach still composing?' Now bear in mind that Bach's dates are 1685–1750 and Gilbert was around in the late nineteenth century. Gilbert replied, 'No, madam, he is decomposing.'

American writer Dorothy Parker (1893–1967), whom we quoted above, is well known for her smart remarks. She is perhaps best remembered for the lines, 'Men seldom make passes/at girls who wear glasses.' This may have dated a bit, but she left a legacy of other witticisms to pick from. On congratulating a woman who had just given birth she wrote, 'We all knew you had it in you.' When Calvin Coolidge (a notably insignificant US

President) died, she asked, 'How could they tell?' Disappointed
at a stage performance by Katherine Hepburn, she wrote in a
review, 'She ran the gamut of the emotions from A to B.' And
when asked what she would like inscribed on her tombstone, she
said, 'This is on me.'

Woody Allen is another writer/performer famous for his smart
remarks. Unlike the idle rich of Wilde's plays, Woody portrays
himself as a poor, neurotic Jew, much put-upon and forever worried about the meaning of life. His movies are peppered with a
variety of witticisms. The first one below is both satiric and allu-
sive. A number of Wagner's operas are about Germanic heroes
and they were supposedly popular with Hitler and the Nazis
(though one has to wonder about that). Allen's light-hearted
remark about Germany's warmongering is black humour.

**I can't listen to that much Wagner. I start getting the urge
to conquer Poland.**

**I was thrown out of college for cheating on the meta-
physics exam. I looked into the soul of the boy sitting
next to me.**

**I took a speed-reading course and I read *War and Peace* in
twenty minutes. It involves Russia.**

While people like Wilde and Allen figure prominently in cata-
logues of witticisms, others have their moments. Sir Robert
Helpmann was once asked what he thought of nude ballet. He
said, 'The trouble is that not everything stops when the music
stops.' Tallulah Bankhead remarked of a play, 'There is less in it
than meets the eye.' Eleanor Roosevelt complained that a rose
named after her was described as 'No good in a bed, but fine up
against a wall.' Presumably we have to thank an anonymous rose
cataloguer for that one.

9

Language in context

Language is not always specific. In normal language use the speaker (or writer or signer) and the addressee are expected to be cooperative. The speaker is expected to be able to estimate what the addressee knows and does not know. If the speaker gives too little information, the addressee will not be able to interpret what was said. If the speaker gives redundant information, the addressee might be confused or insulted. There is an old joke that circulates among children, 'Why do firemen wear red braces?' The answer is, 'To keep their trousers up.' Here the person who poses the question is being uncooperative by including the adjective 'red' and then giving an answer in which colour is irrelevant. Teasing jokes like these are common in books of jokes for children.

In the next example the speaker (the barrister) introduces a redundant adjective 'pregnant' into his question and the addressee (the doctor) goes out of his way to pick up on it.

Barrister: Doctor, how many caesarians have you performed on pregnant women?
Doctor: All my caesarians have been performed on pregnant women.

Estimating what the addressee knows is not always straightforward. We have all had the experience of being insulted by someone telling us something we think is obvious. With children we have expectations of what they are likely to know at a certain age and the order in which they are likely to acquire various words and bits of knowledge. Some humour can be found in cases where children do not conform to our expectations. An acquaintance of mine told me that one of his boys, an eight-year-old, asked if he could watch a television series called *Roots*. The father replied that he could not. The boy asked why. His father told him that he had read a review and it seemed the programme contained a lot of sex and violence. The child appeared to accept this, but after a while he asked, 'What's violence, Dad?' And there was a young girl of about ten who asked her father what a prostitute was. He replied that it was a woman who let men have sex with her for money. She said, 'Oh, you mean a hooker.'

The addressee is expected to behave reasonably and to interpret what is said in terms of what was the most likely intention of the speaker or writer in the context. If someone says, 'Can you pass me that trowel?' and you answer 'Yes', but make no move to get the trowel, either you are being uncooperative or you are making a childish attempt to be funny. It has been common for many years for people filling in forms to be deliberately obtuse. When they come to the box marked 'sex', they write 'Yes, please' and when they come to the question about marital status, they say, 'Fair' or 'Could be better'.

This kind of lack of cooperation figures in a large class of jokes, some of which have much in common with those illustrated in Chapter 1 under 'dashing expectations' and with 'dumb' jokes.

As he paid his hotel bill the guest turned and called to the bellboy, 'Quick, run up to room 225 and see if I left my briefcase. Hurry, please, because I've got just five minutes to catch my train.' Three minutes later, the bellboy was back, all out of breath. 'Yes, sir,' he gasped, 'it's there all right.'

In the next example army recruits have been doing drill for hours under a strict sergeant. One of them has the audacity to speak, and then proves uncooperative.

Recruit: A drowsy numbness pains my sense.
Drill sergeant: Who said that?
Recruit: Keats, wasn't it?

In the next example another recruit has failed to understand a command. He then chooses to put an unlikely interpretation on the sergeant's question.

Sergeant: Don't you know the King's English?
Recruit: Well, I always assumed he was.

There is a story that Mark Twain visited Whistler in his studio and ran his hand over a painting. Whistler rebuked him. 'Please don't touch that painting. The paint isn't dry.' 'That's all right,' said Twain. 'I've got gloves on.' Here Mark Twain manages to avoid the rebuke by pretending to assume Whistler's remark was aimed at saving him from getting paint on his hands.

In the next example the prisoner deliberately misunderstands the judge.

A judge is sentencing a repeat offender. He says, 'I hope this is the last time I'll have to sentence you.' 'Why?' asks the prisoner. 'Are you retiring?'

In the next example we will give the woman the benefit of the doubt. Is she thick or being deliberately obtuse?

A woman with twelve children goes to Social Services.
Interviewer: You have an awful lot of children.
Woman: Well, with twins, you know.
Interviewer: Did you get twins every time?
Woman: Oh, no! Sometimes we got nothing at all.

But I doubt if we would give the benefit of the doubt to A in the next example.

A: My niece got married last Saturday. I had to stand in for my brother who was killed in Iraq.

B: Did you give the bride away?
A: I could have, but I kept my mouth shut.

Variations on the following misinterpretation are common in joke collections.

The manager of a hotel hired a young man to play the piano in the bar. Unfortunately the pianist formed an intimate attachment to the manager's wife. When the manager got wind of this, he thought he would have it out with the pianist, so he went up to him in the bar and said, 'Do you know you've stolen my love?' The pianist replied, 'I'm not sure. Hum a few bars and I'll probably be able to pick it up.'

Language depends on people using commonsense logic, rather than strict logic. It is unreasonable to appeal to a literal, logical reading when there is a normal interpretation available. On the radio you often hear presenters say things like 'My name is Mary Brown until 10 o'clock' or 'Until then I'm John Black.' These statements sound funny if you think about the logic, but the intended meaning is clear. In the next example the young man relies on his boss placing a normal interpretation on what is addressed to him and then presents another possible but unlikely reading.

A young man goes to see his boss. 'Excuse me, sir. Can I have the afternoon off? My wife is going to have a baby.'
'Certainly,' says the boss, 'and good luck.'
When the young man arrives at work next morning, the boss asks him, 'Was it a boy or a girl?'
'Oh, it's too early to tell,' replies the young man. 'It'll take another nine months.'

The difference between strict logic and the kind of inference we might reasonably draw in real life is illustrated by the following exchange in court.

Counsel for the prosecution: Were you intimate with this woman in Edinburgh?
Defendant: I refuse to answer that question.
Counsel for the prosecution: Were you intimate with this woman in Manchester?
Defendant: I refuse to answer that question.
Counsel for the prosecution: Were you intimate with this woman in London?
Defendant: No.

Strictly, we cannot conclude that the defendant was intimate with the woman in question in Edinburgh and Manchester, but since he answered 'no' with respect to London, it is reasonable to assume that he had been.

As mentioned above, language is often ambiguous and relies on the hearer or reader using clues from the context to work out the intended meaning. Brevity leads to ambiguity and places greater onus on the audience. I remember when I was young being puzzled by instructions found in invitations to socials such as *Gentlemen, bring bottle* and *Ladies, bring plate*. It took me some time to work out that neither the bottles nor the plates were meant to be empty. An Indonesian colleague told me that on one occasion he went to meet a friend newly arrived from Indonesia. When he reached the meeting-point, he found his friend sitting on the kerb. When he enquired why his friend was sitting there, the latter pointed to a nearby sign, which read, 'No standing'.

In the following examples there is a sensible interpretation and a nonsensical one.

Toilet closed for repairs. Please use the floor below.

Please don't handle the fruit. Ask for Angie.

Man looking for work. Honest. Will take anything.

Baby was found wrapped in a blanket. Note attached. No name on bottom.

Goods wanted for fête. Get rid of what you don't want. Bring your husband.

10

Errors

A lot of humour is accidental or arises from faulty knowledge of the language. We find someone's mispronunciation funny or their misspelling. Sometimes we are amused by the misuse of words, odd grammar or absurd logic. These errors can also provide the model for jokes.

Slips of the tongue and mispronunciation

We all make slips of the tongue from time to time. Children sometimes transpose sounds within a word so that 'hospital' comes out as *hostipal*. Such transpositions can be imitated in an attempt to be funny as in *Drink will be the urination of me*. The most common type of slip of the tongue is the **spoonerism**, in which corresponding sounds in adjacent words are transposed. The term *spoonerism* is taken from the Reverend William Archibald Spooner, Warden of New College, Oxford (1844–1930), who is alleged to have made frequent slips of the tongue of this type, turning 'You have missed my history lectures' into *You have hissed my mystery lectures*, 'down train' into *town drain*, and 'weary benches' into *beery wenches*. On one occasion he is said to have approached a man sitting in church with the words, *Excuse me, sir. You appear to be occupewing my pie. May I sew you to another sheet?* Not all spoonerisms result in real words, for instance, there is an example of someone turning 'stick in the mud' into *smuck in the tid*, but they often do result in real words and they can be embarrassing. I once tried to say, 'That's a cunning stunt' and produced a four-letter word in conservative company!

An oft-quoted spoonerism, and one that involves parts of a compound word, is *flutterby* for 'butterfly'. It manages to make better sense than the original. Butterflies do flutter by, but it is hard to see any connection between the 'butter' of 'butterfly' and the word 'butter'. One theory is that the word originally referred to butter-coloured varieties.

Spoonerisms and similar transpositions between sounds in neighbouring words are the basis for a lot of light humour. One method is to introduce into the conversation a phrase such as *shining wit* which would be rude if spoonerized. Another is to set up a punchline with a spoonerism, but leave the punchline unspoken.

What's the difference between a cart horse and a war horse?
The war horse darts into the fray...

And of course there's the straight-out spoonerism,

The rabbiter made money by walking his hares.

or the near-spoonerism,

One bird said to the other, 'Bred any good rooks lately?'

Some slips are not transpositions but simply involve the sub-stitution of one sound for another. At one meeting I attended it was decided that we would have to hold an election for office-bearers and we turned towards the female secretary in anticipa-tion of her offer to take care of the details. 'You want me to hold the erection?' she asked in all innocence, and then blushed at her unfortunate mistake.

Freud claimed that slips of the tongue result from repressed notions. The secretary's uttering of *erection* would be interpreted as reflecting her subconscious thinking about such an entity, in other words, she would be thought to have made what has come to be called a 'Freudian slip'. Freud gave many examples to support his contention. For instance, a woman who was on her way to buy castor oil (a much-used laxative in days gone by) for her child said to her companion as she went into the chemist's, 'If you will wait for me for a few movements [moments].' In another instance, a dominant wife said that her sick husband had been to the doctor and 'The doctor said that diet had nothing to do with his ailment and that he could eat and drink anything I want [he wants].' However, there is also evidence that many slips of the tongue are purely the result of malfunctions in forming speech, some configurations of sound being more liable to transposition or substitution than others. In my own speech the vowel of words like *sound* or *house* and the vowel of words like *lawn* and *fawn* tend to transpose if they occur near one another, so a phrase like 'brown horse' is likely to come out as 'brawn house'.

Spoonerisms involve the transposition of sounds, but transpositions of meaningful segments can also occur, as in 'live and *inunterrupted* broadcast' and 'I wonder if they'll *overstand underseas* [understand overseas]', of roots as in 'It keeps people in *animated suspension* [suspended animation] and ' ... *the run-rate would be freeing as flowly as it is in Pakistan*, or even of words as in *They were in great need of an Arabic female-speaking doctor*. All genuine examples.

Besides slips of the tongue there are mispronunciations in the sense of regular pronunciations that are deviant. Since the spelling is such a poor guide to pronunciation in English, there is ample scope for coming up with an odd pronunciation. I know at least two people who have pronounced *bowdlerize* as 'boulderize' until their error was pointed out. This looks like a sort of fossilized spoonerism and may have resulted from a careless reading of the word and substituting the familiar 'boulder' for the obscure 'Bowdler' (the name of the person after whom the process was named). This can easily happen with words first encountered in writing rather than speech.

Small children often have funny pronunciations (funny ha-ha as well as funny peculiar). One child I observed substituted *f* for initial *sm* or *sp* so that 'smile' came out as *file* and 'spot' as *fot*. He also turned 'smart' into *fart*. His parents were thankful that English does not contain a word 'smuck'.

Accents and lisps

Foreign accents have long been a source of jokes. In Chinese there is no 'r' sound, so Chinese speakers with an imperfect control of English sounds will substitute 'l' for 'r'. They are also likely to hear 'r' as 'l', as with the restauranteur Ah So.

A man goes into the restaurant of Ah So and orders calamari. He finds it a bit chewy, so he calls Ah So and says, 'This is rubbery.'
Ah So bows and replies, 'Velly kind of you to say so.'

Conversely, Japanese does not have an 'l' and a Japanese speaker is likely to substitute 'r' and wish you a 'good fright' as you board your plane, or ask everybody to 'crap' when you finish your presentation. These substitutions are natural enough in speech, but I was surprised to find a local Japanese carpenter/cabinet maker with a sign outside his premises advertising 'timber froors'.

One of the neatest examples of exploiting foreign accents I've seen was the slogan adopted by students of speech therapy, who went around wearing tops with the words *Ve haf vays to make you talk*, which plays on the heavy accents used by German WWII baddies in English-language films.

The 'th' sounds of English are difficult for speakers of many languages. In the following joke it is the Italians who are having trouble.

An Italian couple had twins, a girl and a boy. The father knew he had to register the births, but his English was very poor, so he asked his brother to do it. The clerk asked the brother what the name of the little girl was.

'Denise,' he said.
'Very nice. And what is the little boy's name?'
'Denephew.'

Lisping, too, can be a source of humour. The next example is from the 1954 film *Doctor in the House*, the first in what became a successful series of 'Doctor' films. The joke was the source of much comment at the time because it was quite naughty by the standards of the day.

Dirk Bogarde, playing a young doctor, was using his stethoscope on a busty young girl to listen to her breathing. 'Big breaths,' he said. The girl replied, 'Yeth, and I'm only sikth-teen.'

The dropping of initial 'h' is a marked feature of Cockney English and a not infrequent feature of Broad Australian. The following is a true story.

The conservative Prime Minister of Australia in the 1950s, Robert Menzies, was announcing his party's policies at an election rally. A heckler kept interjecting with, 'What are you gonna do about 'ousing?' After he had done this a few times, the Prime Minister broke off from his speech, looked down at him and said, 'Put an 'h' in front of it!'

Non-native speakers of English will always be a potential source of amusement for native speakers, but when the English speakers venture into other languages they are likely to find themselves laughed at. A missionary working in Western Australia began his sermon with what he thought was a good translation into the Western Desert language of 'Believe in the Lord, Jesus Christ, and you shall have everlasting life.' But as soon as he said this, the congregation began to titter. He found out later that he had used *warnka* 'hairy caterpillar' instead of *wanka* 'alive' or 'life', so the people were being promised 'everlasting hairy caterpillars'.

Malapropisms

In Sheridan's eighteenth-century play *The Rivals* there is a character Mrs Malaprop who, in aiming to use certain words, particularly learned ones, frequently uses a *malapropos* or inappropriate substitute (hence the name Sheridan has given her). This is done for humorous effect. At one point she describes someone as 'the very pineapple of politeness' when she presumably means 'the very pinnacle of politeness', and a young woman is said to be 'as headstrong as an allegory on the banks of Nile' (presumably she means 'alligator'). At another point she 'intercedes' [intercepts] a letter in which she is described as an 'old weather-beaten she-dragon' ... who 'deck[s] her dull chat with hard words she don't [sic] understand'. This rouses her to an indignant defence in which she manages four more malapropisms.

> **There, sir, an attack on my language! What do you think of that?—an aspersion upon my parts of speech. Sure, if I reprehend [apprehend] anything in this world it is the use of my oracular [vernacular] tongue, and a nice derangement [arrangement] of epitaphs [epithets]!**

This substitution of a similar word to the one intended has come to be known as a **malapropism** after Sheridan's character. Malapropisms are fairly common, and it is easy to find examples in the speech of politicians, sportscasters and various celebrities. Dan Quayle, US Vice-President in the administration of George Bush the elder and a man not noted for his keen mind, is reported to have said that *Republicans understand the importance of bondage between a mother and child*. George W. Bush (that's the younger one) rivals Mrs Malaprop herself. He talks, for instance, about *preserving powers for his predecessors* and *weapons of mass production*.

A colleague provided me with the following examples from cricket broadcasts:

> **There's a good crowd once again [at the cricket]. It's good to see the contingency from Sri Lanka.**

... Ponting taking an exorbitant pace down the pitch ...

[The bowlers] couldn't eke out [either of the Indian opening batsmen].

[Re a near collision between batsman and bowler]: It wasn't anyone's fault, they both had right of passage.

Other examples from various sources include the church that offers *immorality* [immortality], the resignations that *exasperated* [exacerbated] the staffing situation, the bride with her expensive *torso* [trousseau], people with whom you have an *infinity* [affinity], bushwalkers *clamouring* [clambering] over rocks, Romans who had *vestigial* [Vestal] virgins, and storekeepers taking *infantry* [inventory].

Some errors recur. People frequently *flaunt* [flout] the law, and from time to time they confuse *prostate* and *prostrate*, as in verses 10 and 11 from Psalm 72 reproduced on a church notice sheet. All would have been well if they had stuck to the Authorized Version, where the kings 'fall down before him'.

The Kings of Tarshish and the sea coasts
Shall pay him tribute
The kings of Sheba and Seba
Shall bring him gifts.
Before him all kings shall fall prostate
All nations shall serve him.

Many of these malapropisms are performance errors and the authors would doubtless welcome a chance to correct them. A woman who was impressed by the fact that former students of a Canberra professor held posts in academia and publishing right across Australia said that 'his testicles stretched from Perth to Sydney'. We can be sure she knew the difference between testicles and tentacles. Similarly with the headmaster who was concerned about ruffians mugging his students so he suggested they be trained in the *marital arts*. It is hardly likely that he confused the meanings of *martial* and *marital*. Either he made a slip or, more likely, there was an error in the reporting of his suggestion. However, there are malapropisms that reflect long-term confusion:

* A boy of primary school age was asked where one of his mates went to school. He said *Whiteboilers*. In fact, the school was called 'Whitefriars'. Presumably the unfamiliar 'friars' had been filed away as 'friers' (people who fry) in his lexicon and this led to the substitution of 'boilers'.
* And there was a primary school girl who came home from school and said she had made a new friend and the friend was a *lesbian*. Well, kids are pretty advanced nowadays, but it turned out the girl in question was from Lebanon.
* A press report claimed that someone did not get the sack, but 'resigned of his own fruition' [volition].

Readers can make up their own mind about whether the following are just one-off slips or not.

* A woman returned from a long walk in the country and asked *Is there anything to eat? I'm ravished.* She received a few startled looks. It was assumed that she meant to say 'famished'.
* The following example, which sounds like a mixture of a spoonerism and a malapropism, occurred in an essay on Australian English. The textbook had made mention of Australian speech being characterized by 'pervasive nasality'. The student wrote that it was characterized by *nasal perversity*.

In restaurant reviews I sometimes find the writer talking of having had a *fulsome* meal. Obviously they mean a filling meal. For *fulsome,* dictionaries give meanings such as 'offensive to good taste, gross, disgusting', hardly what was intended. However, when I relate this example to others, I often find that some do not consider it a malapropism, but correct usage! In *Blooming English* Kate Burridge explains that the original meaning was 'abundant' or 'full', but then it came to mean 'over-abundant' or 'excessive', probably because it was associated with the word 'foul'. It is now being used again in something like its original meaning. If enough people use a word in a certain sense, then that becomes a new norm. Perhaps that will happen with *fulsome.*

Something similar to a malapropism can occur with mispronunciation. In social science the subjects who are being tested can be called 'testees'. A non-English speaker reporting her findings pronounced this word with the stress on the first syllable, so that it became homophonous with 'testes'. To make matters worse, she was reporting a survey that grouped subjects in pairs, so there were frequent references to pairs of *testes/testees*.

Non-native speakers can sometimes choose the wrong words with humorous effect, though these examples are not really malapropisms. A Thai newspaper carried a complaint from a man who claimed he was 'hardly beaten' by the police. Since the man was complaining, we can assume he was 'beaten hard'. And finally a story about a Hollywood producer of Hungarian descent who reacted angrily to criticisms of his apparent ignorance with the words, 'You think I know fuck-nothing, but I know fuck-all.'

Malapropisms are sometimes concocted in an attempt to be humorous. Well-worn examples include *pornograph* for 'phonograph' and *What are you incinerating?* for 'What are you insinuating?'

Misinterpretations

Sometimes we misinterpret what we have heard or read, particularly what we have heard. There are essentially two kinds of misinterpretation. In one type the problem is semantic. The hearer or reader does not know a particular word or phrase. I remember at school being confused by the remarkable similarities between Lord Beaconsfield and Disraeli until I found the two names referred to the same person. There is a story about a student who thought Anne Boleyn was an iron. When questioned about this, the student pointed to a passage in the history text, which read, 'Henry, having disposed of Catherine, pressed his suit with Anne Boleyn.' A good story, too good to be true, surely. In the other type of misinterpretation the problem is phonetic. A listener fails to convert the string of sounds into the correct sequence of words. The two types overlap. If one is unfamiliar with certain words or phrases, then one is likely to 'hear' something familiar. There is a new word for such mishearings and it is **mondegreen**. It was coined by Sylvia Wright in *Harper's Magazine* of November 1954, and refers to her mishearing the line of a ballad 'and laid him on the green' as 'and Lady Mondegreen'.

One of the most common misinterpretations is the expanding of *might've* to *might of* instead of *might have*. I had a letter from a professor of linguistics no less, who wrote, 'It might of been better if I had given you the notes myself.'

Religious texts, particularly older translations, frequently contain unfamiliar words and ideas, and these texts are often misinterpreted in odd ways. In the Authorized Version of the Bible (1611) there is the phrase *the quick and the dead*. It means 'the living and the dead', the word *quick* meaning 'living' as in the 'quick of your finger' or 'quicksilver'. Naturally, such a phrase is liable to misinterpretation given that *quick* is no longer in general use as 'living', but is very common with the meaning 'fast'. Not surprisingly *quick* has been changed in more recent translations, but such changes have been too late to prevent generations of misunderstandings. In fact, the phrase *the quick and the dead* is in current use with reference to problems such as trying to cross a busy road.

There is a standard example of a student misinterpreting the Lord's Prayer, writing *Our father, who art in heaven, Harold be thy name*. The story may be apocryphal, but on the other hand one can imagine such an error occurring. The word *hallowed* is not in general use, and there is a general tendency to replace obscure forms with familiar ones. I have the following on good authority: *Everlasting is thy rain* [reign] and *He has spoken through the profits* [prophets]. In these instances, the sound has been picked up correctly, but a homophone has been substituted. Eastman provides another nice example where the archaic past tense of 'to bear' has been misinterpreted.

Shall a mother's tender care
Fail toward the child she-bear?

In some instances it is not clear whether a word has been misinterpreted or simply misspelt. The following is from the words of a hymn displayed on an OHP transparency in a church (supplied by Gavan Breen).

In this world of toil and snares
If I faulter lord who cares.

Someone pointed out to me that children misinterpret the line *Round yon virgin mother and child* in 'Silent Night'. It is understandable that this passage would be obscure to children, particularly with the word *virgin* being there. They take the 'virgin' to be a person separate from the mother and the child, so that in a nativity scene Joseph is taken to be the virgin.

The following example is from a university student. It concerns the last act of *Othello*, where the eponymous hero is stabbing himself to death. He says:

Set you down this:
And say, besides—that in Aleppo once,
Where a malignant and a turban'd Turk
Beat a Venetian and traduc'd the state,
I took by the throat the circumcised dog,
And smote him—thus.

The phrase *circumcised dog* refers to the Turk, who, being Muslim, would have been circumcised. The student, failing to see that this phrase referred to the Turk, wrote that in Aleppo Othello stabbed a Turk's circumcised dog. This also raises the question of why someone would circumcise a dog. Come to think of it, why would anyone circumcise a human?

Some student errors are quite understandable. One student was asked to write from memory part of the Song of Solomon. In the Authorized Version, verse 12 of chapter 2 is as follows: *The flowers appear on the earth; the time of the singing of birds is come, and the voice of the turtle is heard in our land.* However, the student wrote *the voice of the tortoise.* Now for most people *tortoise* and *turtle* are synonyms, but these creatures don't have voices that are prominent in spring. Obviously *turtle* here refers to *turtle dove*. It is interesting to reflect on how the student had interpreted the text, and one wonders how many others had done likewise. It is common when referring to taboo areas such as sex and 'the natural functions' to use euphemisms, or 'nice' expressions. These euphemisms can easily be misunderstood. Euphemisms have been much used in the law, where the penis is referred to as the 'arm', 'the yard' or even, as in the following instance, 'the person'. The story is about a case of indecent exposure where the witness was not too sharp on picking up on the attorney's euphemisms.

Attorney for the prosecution: Did you see the defendant's person?
Witness (completely baffled): What?
Attorney for the prosecution: Did you see the defendant's ...?
Witness: Yes, I did.
Attorney for the prosecution: Can you tell the court what state it was in?
Witness: Iowa.
Attorney for the prosecution: No, no. Which way was it pointing?
Witness: Towards Des Moines.

In Chapter 1, I mentioned a category of jokes where a learned term is deliberately misunderstood. Here is a well-known joke about someone's genuine failure to understand an unfamiliar technical term.

A woman tells her neighbour that she is very worried about her son. She has taken him to a psychiatrist and the psychiatrist has told her that he has an Oedipus complex. The neighbour tries to reassure her, 'Oedipus schmoedipus! What does it matter? As long as he's a good boy and loves his mother.'

Misspellings

For the last hundred years or so we have had standardized spelling in English, two standards to be exact, based on the *Oxford English Dictionary* and *Webster's Dictionary* in the USA. All published materials should conform to one or other of these standards, but private correspondence contains spelling errors, as do many student assignments and amateur postings on the web. In these you are likely to find anything from the odd error to a text where there are several errors per sentence. Misspelling is understandable in English. We have easily the worst relationship between sound and spelling of any language in the world.

Most misspellings are of little interest. However, sometimes they demonstrate a confusion of one word for another, a kind of misinterpretation rather like those in the previous section. Some of these misspellings are understandable. I remember hesitating over 'surname' (was it *sir name,* somehow connected with sir?), and I recently heard someone criticized for writing 'hold your piece' instead of 'hold your peace', but I must admit I had often wondered whether the expression referred to a piece of dialogue as in 'say one's piece'. Some expressions cry out to be misinterpreted. There is a proverbial expression, 'When all fruit fails, welcome the haws.' Now *haw* is not a common word, so it is no surprise that when a class was asked to write this expression from dictation, some wrote, 'When all fruit fails, welcome the whores.' But even making allowances for understandable confusion about connections between words, it is hard not to be amused by some spelling errors that make an unwarranted association between words, as in the case of the man who was 'not being phased by setbacks', the pig-shooter who was in 'danger of being attacked by mature bores', the motel that boasted all its meals 'were cooked on the premise', and the defence against a charge of violence that claimed the act was the result of 'deep-seeded cultural morays [mores]'.

One student wrote, 'She wore a red belt around her waste' (sounds as if she should have gone on a diet), another wrote, 'The city was raised to the ground' (where did he think the city was before it was raised?), and a third wrote, 'Estate agents are always wringing my mother', which gives rise to disturbing images. Interestingly, estate agents are among the worst offenders when it comes to spelling. They frequently use *compliment* instead of *complement*, usually in contexts such as 'The garden *compliments* the house.' As a friend of mine says, it sounds as if the garden is saying, 'What a nice house you are!' One interesting example of misspelling was reported to me from a church notice. It read, 'The choir has a number of fine sinners.' Choir practice must have been fun!

There is also a famous example of misspelling from Dan Quayle. On one occasion he was helping at a spelling bee for schoolchildren. In the process he managed to 'correct' one child's *potato*, turning it into *potatoe*.

While it is clear that Vice-president Quayle made an error in spelling, it is not always obvious whether an error is just a slip in spelling or a reflection of a long-term misinterpretation of the type illustrated a few pages back. Presumably *Minister for the Rats* (Arts) is a misspelling and so is *The gamekeeper was supposed to stop people shooting the peasants* and *Personnel working in the pubic sector*, but the following could be long-term misunderstandings like those illustrated in the previous section.

Alleluia, Alleluia! A great profit has appeared among us; God has visited his people. Alleluia! [church handout]

My flesh Israel food and my blood real drink. [church handout]

A family whose young child was scolded after water discharged from a solar hot water overflow system saw immediate action from within the trade sector [newspaper].

He was self-scented and cared little about the feelings of others.

A wife should be understanding and bare with her husband.

Deliberate misspelling is sometimes used for humorous effect. Graham Rawle devised a series of cartoons for the *Weekend Guardian* with captions in which a consonant was lost to give a very different interpretation, for instance: *His solicitor sent him a copy of the d[r]aft contract*. There is an extended example of misspelling in Dickens's *Great Expectations* where young Pip's letter to Joe Gargery is full of childish errors. A few writers have adopted systematic misspelling. These include the American humourists Artemus Ward (1834–67) and Josh Billings (1818–85), both of whom often wrote a kind of home-made philosophy, and the deviant spelling suggested some kind of rural sage. I will attempt to give some examples from Billings, no easy task given the assiduous attempts of my spell-checker to correct Mr Billings's writing.

Chastity iz like an isikel. If it onse melts that's the last ov it.

It iz tru that welth won't maik a man vartuous, but I notis thare ain't ennybody who wants tew be poor jist for the purpiss ov being good.

There are a number of books illustrating varieties of English written wholly in misspelling. The spelling is phonetic in that it deviates from convention in the direction of pronunciation, but additionally it moves word breaks rather arbitrarily for comic effect. Here are two examples. The first is from *Let Stalk Strine* by Afferbeck Lauder and represents an attempt to capture the Australian accent. The exchange concerns a lady's request for a tomato sandwich and a ham and pickle sandwich.

A: Sell semmithches?
B: Air, emeny jiwant?
A: Gimme utter martyr and an airman pickle. Emma chisit?
B: Toon ninepen slidy.

The second is from *Fraffly Well Spoken: How to Speak the Language of London's West End* by the same author. The speaker is not quite sure that she quite agrees 'with all you say',

Em nogwet shorrif egg-wetter gree withol you sair, but ashel defend to your death may rate to say so.

Sometimes a misspelling is used as a pun, as in a report on a husband attempting to stab his wife's lover with a rapier that was headed *A sworded tale*. Business names, advertisements and signs often employ deliberate misspellings to attract attention. One fast food outlet is called *Frier Tuck's*.

Nowadays most published texts are prepared on a computer and there is a spelling check available (as mentioned above). However, although the spell-check will pick up errors such as a-c-c-o-m-o-d-a-t-i-o-n for 'accommodation', it will not pick up cases where the misspelling coincides with another word. The lesson is *Know won can trussed there spell cheque*. Some typographical errors are probably misprints rather than misspellings. For instance, if a printed text contains the sentence 'The wound turned *sceptic*', you can't tell whether the writer has confused the words *septic* and *sceptic* or whether the two similar words have been confused in the typing. Those errors that result from the omission of words are clearly misprints. An early edition of the Bible omitted 'not' from one of the commandments. You can guess which one. It was probably a Freudian misprint. Readers were told, 'Thou shalt commit adultery.'

Mispunctuation

Punctuation in writing corresponds pretty well with the grouping of words in speech, so there can be humour based on misgrouping that shows up in inappropriate phrasing in speech or inappropriate punctuation in writing. Compare *What is this thing called love?* and *What is this thing called, love?* or *Well, I must get on, my dear old friend* and *Well, I must get on my dear old friend*.

There is an example featured in a number of websites that presents the sequence *A woman without her man is nothing*. It can be punctuated to give two entirely different meanings:

Woman without her man is nothing.
Woman, without her, man is nothing.

In speech parenthetical clauses can be marked as such by intonation or pauses, and these pauses should be marked by commas in writing. However, this is not always done, and the presence or absence of commas can change the force of a relative clause.

Convent girls who have sex with boys need to be given instruction in safe sex.
Convent girls, who have sex with boys, need to be given instruction in safe sex.

In the sentence without commas we take the *who*-clause to be picking just those girls who have managed to snare a boy from the Jesuits across the road, but in the sentence with the commas the *who*-clause refers to all the convent girls, a most unlikely situation, even in these permissive times.

The apostrophe is interesting. Historically, it marked the possessive form of a noun as in *lady's handbag*, *child's toy*, but there is a problem if you want to write the plural of an alphabetism like *cv* for *curriculum vitae* (the academic's résumé). If one writes *cvs*, it looks as if three words have been abbreviated, so one writes *cv's*. Some people seem to have a problem with the plural of certain words of foreign extraction ending in a vowel. A word like *logo* will look like the Greek word *logos* without an apostrophe, so it becomes *logo's*. The next step is the greengrocer's apostrophe, which is used in any plural: *bean's*, *cucumber's* and *potatoe's* (a spelling that led Dan Quayle astray). A sign on a housing development near my university invites people to *Live among the tree's*, in recognition of the four or five trees found on the estate. Not much scope for humour with the apostrophe, one would have thought, but one newspaper managed a nice example in a review of an episode of the TV detective series *Dalziel and Pascoe*. The episode was called *Mens sana*, short for the Latin motto *mens sana in corpore sano* 'A healthy mind in a healthy body'. The review was headed *Men's Sana*, which made it sound like something akin to the 'men's sauna'. There is also an example from Northern Ireland where the greengrocer's apostrophe was inserted in the following anti-Catholic piece of graffiti *Mick's out*. Someone added, 'But he'll be back after lunch.' An apostrophe can be critical to the sense, as in the following.

Should I sleep with my wife or the prince's, I wonder.
Should I sleep with my wife or the princes, I wonder.

With the apostrophe my choice lies between my wife and the princess. Without the apostrophe, my choice lies between my wife and a number of princes. Whatever turns you on!

Grammar as she is spoke

We don't all speak the same way. We don't all have the same grammar. But most of us have some kind of notion of correct grammar, and deviations from that norm can be irritating, or in the following case, amusing. I heard this father–son dialogue over the back fence when I was living in Sydney in the late 1960s. An unusual plane had just flown overhead and dad wanted to know if his son had witnessed this significant event.

Father: Did you see that?
Son: Yes, daddy, I seed it.
Father (in mock horror): What?
Son: Daddy, I sawed it.
Father (more mock horror): What?
Son: Daddy, I seen it.
Father: That's better.

The father had a clear idea of what was right and what was wrong, but his notion of correct grammar was definitely non-standard. There are jokes in the literature based on a non-standard regularized past tense of 'see'. A woman says to her servant, 'Did you seed the grapefruit?' The servant replies, 'Yes, ma'am, I seed it. It's right over there.'

Some one-off innovations are amusing. A cricket commentator said the match *ebb and flowed*, taking 'ebb and flow' as if it were a single word. A child, who was asked to look for his father's watch, replied, 'I'll look for it, daddy. I'll peel my eyes', that is, keep my eyes peeled. And a radio personality asked listeners to 'Keep your ears peeled back.'

In 1963 President Kennedy visited the Berlin Wall. Wanting to show empathy, he tried to say in German 'I am a Berliner'. Unfortunately, he translated the English literally and produced *Ich bin ein Berliner*. It would have fine without *ein*. As it came out, it means 'I am a type of bun', just as *Ich bin ein Frankfurter* would have meant 'I am a type of sausage'.

Logic or lack thereof

Lack of clear thinking can result in humour. It can be a matter of vacuity or redundancy, circularity or paradox.

Let us start with a few examples where there is the whiff of vacuity or redundancy, i.e. where certain words don't seem to be worth saying. Consider the following exchange between a barrister and a witness. On the face of it the barrister's second question is redundant since the witness is still alive, but this question and its answer might serve to minimize the evidence against the accused.

Counsel for the defence: He threatened to kill you?
Witness: That is correct.
Counsel for the defence: Did he in fact kill you?
Witness: No.

However, it is not always so easy to find justification for apparent redundancy. The child of a friend of mine was given a set of small tiles bearing letters of the alphabet. The box carried a warning, 'Letters may be used to construct words, phrases and sentences that may be deemed offensive.' Presumably we are not meant to take *may* in the permissive sense; the manufacturer wants us to be aware of the possibility of a child making up a sequence such as B, U and M or worse. But surely this is obvious, and even in these litigious times, it is hard to imagine a po-faced parent suing the manufacturer because their beloved offspring put together a four-letter word.

Some years ago someone gave me a kind of pressure pack with a tube that could be connected to the valve on a car tyre. It is designed to blow up a partially deflated tyre. Now I can imagine someone not knowing what it is for, but surely the admonition on the can 'Not to be used for breast augmentation' is superfluous. Just as bad, in fact, as the first aid directions for treating burns which began with 'First remove the victim from the fire.'

False logic can be a source of humour. In the following example a student is trying to relate something about the disputed authorship of Shakespeare's plays. I am not sure if it is authentic. I have seen a number of very similar examples in lists of howlers.

The plays were not written by Shakespeare, but by someone else of the same name.

Young children often provide examples of curious logic, as in the following case where a boy aged four visited a neighbour and witnessed her breast-feeding her baby. This is the exchange with his mother that took place when he came home:

Child: Mrs Jones doesn't get milk from a bottle for her baby. She has pumps in her chest, and she pumps milk into the baby.
Mother: Don't you remember when your little brother was fed that way?
Child: Oh, did you send him into Mrs Jones?

It is not only children who exhibit unclear thinking. In 1972 when university students were revolting (aren't they always?), some of them wanted to abolish exams, and a few wanted to abolish the concept of 'fail', because, they said, 'failure had negative connotations'. Although this seems amusing to me, it is a serious matter for some people still today. At a recent teachers' conference there was a debate about whether to abolish the notion of failure. Apparently one can still lose a match or run unplaced, but one cannot fail.

I once read a report from a health worker commenting on the death of a patient, in which it was stated that 'the health of the patient deteriorated to such an extent that death was the only viable option'. The health worker had presumably lost sight of the fact that viable means 'able to live'. A similar ignorance probably lies behind the sentence *The spectators were literally glued to their seats*. The writer was not reporting a prankster's use of Superglue, but probably thought the word *literally* expressed some degree of emphasis.

A correspondent to a newspaper complaining about streakers demanded they be *exposed*, and another writing in favour of capital punishment wrote that *Capital punishment recognizes the sanctity of human life*. I would assume that the writers in these cases knew the meaning of the words they were using, but were insensitive to the irony in what they were writing.

The next example is from someone in the USA who forgot that audiences do not normally include dead people. He said to his audience, 'I don't know anyone here who was killed with a handgun.' This is similar to a comment attributed to the boxer Alan 'Boom Boom' Minter, one-time world middleweight champion, 'Sure, there have been injuries and deaths in boxing, but none of them serious.'

Sportspersons and sports commentators are good sources of faulty logic, redundancy, and vacuity. A newly appointed American basketball coach was quoted as saying that he would turn the team around 360 degrees. He must have been away the day they did geometry. And soccer player Ian Rush is credited, if that's the word, with having said, 'Moving from Wales to Italy is like moving to another country.' The next examples are from sports broadcasts:

I can give you the result in one word: protest dismissed.

Well, it's Ipswich 0 and Liverpool 2. If that's the way the score stays, then you've got to favour Liverpool to win.

And in comes Bob Taylor, looking very distinguished with his grey hair, which you can't see because it's completely covered by his helmet.

What a great day it has been since the sun went down.

So this is her fifth match point, or the fifth time she's had match point.

I suppose there's no reason why sports stars and commentators should be clear thinkers and competent in language, but it would be nice to think that politicians were. In fact, politicians are regular offenders, and some of the most powerful men in the world are the worst offenders. If I told you that a minister thought that the London Underground was a political movement, you would think it was a joke, and you'd be right. But a certain foreign minister dealing with the Middle East thought the West Bank was a financial institution. No joke.

Mussolini's Fascist government was keen on preserving the purity of Italian and at one stage it tried to ban foreign words by using posters with the order *Boicottate le parole stranieri* 'Boycott foreign words'. As you can see, the prohibition itself uses the English word *boycott*.

Margaret Thatcher once came out with, 'As God once said, and I think rightly ...' No error here, but an interesting revelation of her self-perception. Here are some more examples of unfortunate utterances from politicians.

I'd like the taxes to go to those parents lucky enough to have children.

No one would go to Hitler's funeral if he were alive today.

We're sending 23 million leaflets to every household in Britain.

Sir Thomas More, as well as a politician, was also a thinker.

I'm a great fan of baseball. I watch a lot of games on the radio.

Gerald Ford

It's no exaggeration to say the undecideds could go one way or the other.

George Bush, 1988

I stand for anti-bigotry, anti-semitism and anti-racism.

George Bush, 1988

And Dan Quayle, always a good contributor to collections of linguistic oddities, provided the following:

My friends, no matter how rough the road may be, we can and we will, never, never surrender to what is right.

If we do not succeed, then we run the risk of failure.

We are ready for any unforeseen event that may or may not occur.

I love California. I practically grew up in Phoenix.

We are going to have the best-educated American people in the world.

These slips are interesting in the context of other errors. It is not uncommon for speakers or writers to accidentally say the opposite of what they intend, as with Bush's anti-semitism and Quayle's never surrendering to what is right. One newspaper wrote of 'a new era of co-operation in the fight against third world health' and a radio station said that someone's contribution could not be 'underestimated'. Another radio station announced that 'They [the Chinese] have lost one chance of hosting the Olympics; they're not going to let anything get in the way of losing another.'

Lack of logic is the basis of a lot of 'dumb' jokes (see Chapter 7). Here is a variation on that theme. In *The Goon Show*, a 1950s programme of nonsense provided by Spike Milligan, Peter Sellers and Harry Secombe, a man on safari hears the sound of a boot being removed and dropped on the floor. 'Must be the one-legged man in the tent upstairs taking his boot off.' The same sound is heard again. 'Must be two one-legged men in the tent upstairs taking their boot off.'

The following is similar, pure nonsense, unlikely even to have come from the lips of a television personality.

Didn't I meet you in Seattle?
No. I've never been to Seattle.
Neither was I. It must have been two other chaps.

Mark Twain is the source of the next example,

We were identical twins. One of us drowned.
Some think it was Bill. Some think it was me.

And here is another 'illogical' joke, this time from Marilyn Monroe in *Some Like It Hot*,

Real diamonds! They must be worth their weight in gold.

I wonder what she would have said if someone had offered her second-hand diamonds.

11

Rhymes

Some words alliterate, that is, they share an initial consonant or consonant cluster, as with *flame*, *flicker* and *flutter*. Some words rhyme, as with *cat*, *sat* and *mat*. Words of more than one syllable have a certain stress pattern. The words *divinity* and *vicinity* share the same stress pattern as well as rhyming. All cultures exploit rhythm, and many use alliteration or rhyme as well, in chants, poems and lyrics.

Pre-school children often delight in exploring features such as rhyme and they like to recite catchy pieces of verse. School-children not only recite rhymes, but invent new ones from time to time, including parodies of existing rhymes. Some years ago young people used to take their leave with a rhyming expression *See you later, alligator*, which would elicit a rhyming reply *In a while, crocodile*. These were taken from a popular song of the day by Bill Haley and His Comets.

Formal features of language such as metre and rhyme are used for serious poetry, of course, but in this book we confine our attention to light and humorous verse. In this genre rhythms are preferred where a number of unstressed syllables come between each stressed syllable. This achieves a light and breezy tone. If the rhyme (in the sense of the actual rhyming bit) runs from a stressed syllable over a few unstressed syllables, quite a catchy effect can be achieved, as in the following example from a patter song by W. S. Gilbert in *The Pirates of Penzance*.

Here's a first-rate opportunity
To get married with impunity,
And indulge in the felicity
Of unbounded domesticity.
You shall quickly be parsonified,
Conjugally matrimonified,
By a doctor of divinity,
Who resides in this vicinity.

In general speech it is considered inappropriate to rhyme, and if one accidentally comes out with a rhyme, someone usually comments on it. In fact, there is an idiomatic expression for this purpose, *You're a poet and don't know it*. One of the functions of rhyme is mnemonic. Children are taught the following rhyme to learn the names of the evangelists.

Matthew, Mark, Luke and John,
Hold the horse while I get on.

And I still have to recite to myself the following rhyme when trying to remember how many days in a month.

Thirty days hath September,
April, June and November.

A piece of traditional wisdom encapsulated in rhyme and one I still encounter from time to time is the following.

A red sky in the morning
Is a shepherd's warning.
A red sky at night
Is a shepherd's delight.

Rhyming slogans and war cries designed to be chanted are popular with demonstrators, schools, some sports teams and their supporters. Demonstrators, for instance, chant lines such as,

This is not a police state.
We've the right to demonstrate.

The chants of schools and minor sporting teams are usually of little entertainment value and quite innocuous. Not so the songs and chants of British football teams, to judge from the examples on the web. These seem to manage to combine racism, sexism, blasphemy, homophobia and general grossness.

Besides rhymes in the sense of poems, there are also rhyming words and expressions such as *bigwig* 'important person', *mop chop* 'haircut', *hocus-pocus* 'nonsense, trickery', *hanky-panky* 'illicit sexual intimacy', *itsy-bitsy* 'small, insignificant', *mumbo-jumbo* 'disparaging term for unintelligible text, especially jargon' and *roly-poly*. *Roly-poly* is used of a kind of tumbleweed, and for a rumour that gets bigger the further it travels. It is also used for a rolled suet pudding, and a fat person can be described as 'roly-poly'. English uses something similar to rhyme to express oscillation; for instance, the following words have the same consonants in each constituent but the vowel alternates: *flip-flop*, *ding-dong*, *tick-tock* and *wig-wag*. There is also a rhyming practice found mainly in American English, and derived from Yiddish, of adding *schm-* to the repetition of a word to form a rhyme. Examples include *answer-schmanser* and *offer-schmoffer*. See the Oedipus-Schmoedipus joke under 'Misinterpretations'. Other rhyming expressions that have some entertainment value include the following:

Bi-guy: a bisexual

Chalk and talk: traditional method of teaching

Cell yell [US]: talking loudly on a cell [mobile] phone

Chick flick : a movie aimed at female audiences

Cuddle puddle: spa bath

Culture vulture: someone keen on highbrow culture

Fag hag: female who goes around with gay men

Gangbang: a number of males having intercourse with a female

Hi-fi: high fidelity (reproduction of sound)

Nipple cripple: pinching someone's nipple (usually a male's) to cause pain

Pooper scooper: a tool for picking up doggy doings

Rich bitch: pejorative term for a female with money

Shaggin' wagon: a vehicle, usually a van, used as a venue for sex

Silly billy: term applied to an addressee who has committed some small act of folly

Sin bin: a rugby player who offends is sent off the field to the sin bin (also an alternative to *shaggin' wagon*)

Snail mail: ordinary mail as opposed to e-mail

Trailer sailer: a type of small yacht that can be easily towed by car

There is a widespread belief that sportsmen should refrain from sex before important games. A witty term for this practice is recorded by Gerry Wilkes in his *Dictionary of Australian Colloquialisms*, where we find that players are instructed to sleep *bum to mum*.

Nursery rhymes

There are some scores of widely known rhymes which parents teach their children. They are known as *nursery rhymes* in English-speaking countries and *Mother Goose songs* in the USA. (Oops! Sorry about that!) Here is a well-known one.

Ride a cock-horse to Banbury Cross,
To see a fine lady upon a white horse;

With rings on her fingers and bells on her toes,
She shall have music wherever she goes.

Like most nursery rhymes this one is anonymous. Another popular nursery rhyme is 'Little Miss Muffet'.

Little Miss Muffet
Sat on a tuffet,
Eating her curds and whey.
Along came a spider
Who sat down beside her
And frightened Miss Muffet away.

I once had to enrol a female student with the surname *Muffet*. On spotting her name on her enrolment form, I remarked, 'Ah, Little Miss Muffet.' Then, after a pause, I added, 'I suppose everyone says that.' Miss Muffet replied, 'Yes, and then everyone says THAT.'

Another favourite nursery rhyme is 'Mary Had a Little Lamb'. This is not 'anonymous' as most traditional rhymes are. It was written by Sarah Hale, of Boston, in 1830.

Mary had a little lamb,
Its fleece was white as snow;
And everywhere that Mary went,
The lamb was sure to go.

It followed her to school one day,
Which was against the rule;
It made the children laugh and play,
To see a lamb at school.

As testimony to the popularity of this nursery rhyme, witness the numerous parodies that have been produced, some of which are given below.

Children's verses

Besides nursery rhymes there are rhymes that circulate among children. Many of them are 'rude' and children would not normally recite them in front of parents or teachers. Some rhymes accompany skipping or games. The following rhyme, 'Oranges and Lemons', is used in a game where two players stand opposite each other joining hands and holding them high. As they recite the rhyme, other participants file through the arch formed by their raised arms. As they finish the last line, and the number of repetitions of 'head' is somewhat arbitrary, they bring down their arms and capture someone. This procedure is repeated until everyone has been captured and is followed by a tug-of-war. The first version below is the one I encountered as a child. The second is one of a number of longer versions that list many London churches. *Bow*, for instance, is St Mary-le-Bow, which, according to legend, tolled the message 'turn again' to Dick Whittington as he stood on Parliament Hill to take a last look before leaving London. St Clement's is either St Clement's, Cheapside, or St Clement Danes. Note that *farthings* was once pronounced *fartins* and would have rhymed with *Martins*.

Oranges and lemons,
Sing the bells of St Clemens.
I owe you a farthing.
When shall I pay you?
Today or tomorrow?
Chip, chop, the last man's head,
Head, head ... off!

* *

Oranges and lemons,
Say the bells of St Clement's.
You owe me five farthings,
Say the bells of St Martin's.

When will you pay me?
Say the bells of Old Bailey.
When I grow rich,
Say the bells of Shoreditch.
When will that be?
Say the bells of Stepney.
I do not know,
Says the great bell of Bow.
Here comes a candle
To light you to bed.
Here comes a chopper
To chop off your head.
Chip, chop, chip, chop.
The last man's head, head ... off!

Other schoolyard rhymes have other purposes. For instance, there is a rhyme to dispel rain, which probably originates in adult incantations for the same purpose,

Rain, rain, go away.
Come again another day.
Little Johnny wants to play.

The next is recited to anyone whose shirt is hanging out, once the normal state after playtime, and nowadays the preferred mode full stop.

Dicky, Dicky Dout,
Your shirt's hanging out,
Five miles in and five miles out.

Others are just for fun, as with this parody of the *Bridal March*.

Here comes the bride
All fat and wide,
She cannot get in the front door,
She has to get in the side.

Parodies are common in children's repertoires. There are a number of parodies of the first stanza of Felicia Hemans's poem 'Casabianca' (not Casablanca!). This was a popular poem about a boy, Casabianca, who remained at his post in the Battle of the Nile. I give the original first.

The boy stood on the burning deck
Whence all but he had fled;
The flame that lit the battle's wreck
Shone round him o'er the dead.

****

The boy stood on the burning deck
Picking his nose like mad,
And rolling it up in little balls,
And throwing it at his dad.

As mentioned above, there are numerous parodies of 'Mary Had a Little Lamb'.

Mary had a little lamb,
She also had a bear.
I've often seen her little lamb,
But I've never seen her bare.

Mary had a little lamb,
You've heard the tale before,
But did you know she passed her plate
And had a little more?

Adult verses

Writing light, humorous verse is fairly common, but not easy to do well. Edward Lear and Lewis Carroll are well-known exponents from the nineteenth century. An example of Lear's verse appears under 'Limericks' below. Thomas Hood (1799–1845) was another who wrote humorous verse. The following is the last stanza of 'Faithless Sally Brown', which contains a couple of nice puns.

His death, which happened in his berth,
    At forty-odd befell:
They went and told the sexton, and
    The sexton toll'd the bell.

Hood had a social conscience and much of his writing is serious, but he sometimes used comic verse to make a serious point. The following is the first stanza of 'Faithless Nelly Gray'.

Ben Battle was a soldier bold,
    And used to war's alarms;
But a cannon-ball took off his legs,
    So he laid down his arms.

C. S. Calverley (1831–84) wrote comic verse, especially about courting. The following is an example of a comic alphabet in verse form—a minor genre, which flourished in the nineteenth century.

A is an Angel of blushing eighteen:
B is the Ball where the Angel was seen:
C is her Chaperone, who cheated at cards:
D is the Deuxtemps, with Frank of the Guards:
E is the Eye which those dark lashes cover:
F is the Fan it peeped wickedly over:
G is the Glove of superlative kid:
H is the Hand which it spitefully hid:

Humorous rhymes are still fairly popular in an age that has practically given up reading poetry. There are a number of anonymous examples in circulation, such as the following.

Give a thought for signwriter Joe,
He fell to his death while painting an O.
The way of his going
Could not have been better.
He went as he came,
Through a hole in a letter.

Probably the best-known writer of humorous verse in the twentieth century was Ogden Nash (1902–71). Many of his verses are short and quite a few are about creatures, as with the next pithy example.

The Cow
The cow is of the bovine ilk;
One end is moo, the other milk.

Among humorous rhymes are to be numbered bawdy verses. Most of these are X-rated and go out of their way to be as dirty as possible. Well-known examples include 'Abdul Abulbul Emir', 'The Good Ship Venus' and 'The Ballad of Eskimo Nell'. Here is one of the more printable stanzas of 'Eskimo Nell'.

Now they knew the fame of our hero's name
From the Horn to Panamá.
So with nothing worse than a muttered curse
Those dagos sought the bar.
And the women too his habits knew
Down there on the Rio Grande,
So forty whores whipped down their drawers
At Deadeye Dick's command.

Limericks

The five-line limerick is by far the best-known form used for humorous verse. It came into currency in Ireland in the early nineteenth century and became popular in England around the middle of the same century. The first line follows the formula

There was a [person] *from a particular* [place]. This 'place' provides the basis for the rhyme in lines two and five. Lines three and four rhyme with one another, so the overall rhyming schema is *aabba*.

Edward Lear (1812–88) came to prominence as a writer of light verse with the publication of a volume of limericks entitled *A Book of Nonsense* in 1846. He achieved the rhyme in the last line by repeating the name of the subject from line one, an easy way for a writer to find a rhyme.

There was an Old Person of Ewell,
Who chiefly subsisted on gruel;
But to make it more nice
He inserted some mice,
Which refreshed that Old Person of Ewell.

Here are two well-known anonymous limericks. The first is a little unusual in using *tiger* twice in the rhyme, rather like Edward Lear's use of the same word in the first and last lines.

There was a young lady of Riga,
Who went for a ride on a tiger;
They returned from the ride
With the lady inside,
And a smile on the face of the tiger.

There was a young lady of Bright,
Who could travel much faster than light,
She started one day
In a relative way,
And came back the previous night.

The next example is clever in working a number of question-words into the line. In normal prose these come at the beginning of a question (Who has the right? What do you want to do? With what will you do it? To whom will you do it?).

There was a young queer from Khartoum,
Who took a dyke up to his room.
They argued all night
Over who had the right
To do what and with what and to whom.

The next (anonymous) example is notable for its imperfect rhyme (check it out!).

There was a young curate from Kidderminster,
Who inadvertently chid a spinster.
While on the ice
She said words that weren't nice
When he accidentally slid against her.

Clerihews

The clerihew is a humorous verse of four lines. The first and second lines rhyme, as do the third and fourth. The subject is normally a person, usually someone famous, whose name appears at the end of the first line. There is no real metre; a clerihew is rather like prose with rhyme. It was invented by Edmund Clerihew Bentley (1875–1956), also well known as the author of the first modern crime novel, *Trent's Last Case* (1913). He published three volumes of this verse form, in 1905, 1929 and 1939. Here is a typical example from Bentley himself.

It was a weakness of Voltaire's
To forget to say his prayers,
And one which to his shame
He never overcame.

Clerihews are often asked for in literary competitions, and usually combine mockery of the famous with playful language and rhyme. Here are some modern examples.

Intellectual Germaine Greer
Used to drink Aussie beer.
Now she writes on women,
But her powers are dimmin'.

Clerihew writer E. C. Bentley
Played with words rather gently.
He was a master of rhyme,
Which real men thought a waste of time.

Verse today

Reading traditional verse has been in decline over the course of the twentieth century, but other forms of verse have become popular including rap lyrics and SMS verse. The *Guardian*'s first text poetry competition attracted over 7000 entries. Some of these text verses are humorous, or at least seem cute to outsiders unfamiliar with their use of abbreviations.

I no u r gr8t
So I cn hardly w8t
2 come 2 yr place
& c u f2f.

12

Beyond a joke

In my Introduction I pointed out how pervasive humour is, but humour is just part of the larger phenomenon of playing with words, which takes in word games like Scrabble, anagrams, palindromes and acrostics on the one hand, and oblique, obscure and secret language on the other.

There is a certain obscurity built into language when you consider idioms such as 'raining cats and dogs', where the meaning of the expression is not transparent from the words. There are also obscure expressions we use in certain circumstances. I remember as a child being intrigued by the question 'Is your father a glazier?' addressed to someone blocking one's view. I had no idea what a glazier was, and it was some years before I understood that the implication was, 'Do you think you are made of glass? Please move. I can't see through you.'

We normally think of language as a means of exchanging information, and it is. But an enormous amount of language use involves being indirect. How often do we use sarcasm, mocking irony, colourful exaggeration, euphemism, and insincere flattery, to say nothing of straight-out lying.

Many people have reason to restrict their communication to certain persons. Besides the obvious examples of governments and corporations with their secret codes and ciphers, there are so-called secret languages of the Pig Latin type, once popular among schoolchildren, where words are systematically distorted to keep communication secret from parents, teachers or kids not 'in the know'. There are also forms of argot, special slang vocabularies, used by criminals and others who want to be able to communicate without being understood by the authorities. Rhyming slang, which involves replacing a word with a rhyming phrase such as *apples and pears* for 'stairs', is a well-known example of something akin to an argot. Although to some extent it has come into general use, it started off among those whose activities aroused the interest of the police. It can be made more obscure by omitting the rhyming word; for instance, referring to 'the phone' as *the dog* instead of *the dog and bone*.

Obscurity and wit can overlap, which is not surprising when you consider that almost any joke involves leading the audience in a false direction in order to spring a surprise. Modern riddles are a good example, where obscurity and humour combine. The traditional riddle was not humorous, just obscure. Heroes in folklore were often confronted with riddles or conundrums such as the one posed by the Oracle at Thebes and reputedly solved by Oedipus.

What animal is it that in the morning goes on four feet, at noon on two, and in the evening upon three?

The answer would appear to be so obvious that it is hard to believe it remained unsolved until Oedipus came along, but it does illustrate the nature of the traditional riddle. The modern riddle is usually found in children's joke books or Christmas crackers and it involves a pun or similar play on words.

What did Mrs Cook say when Captain Cook died?
That's the way the cookie crumbles.

Clues to cryptic crosswords are obscure by definition, but they are often clever and sometimes witty as well. For instance, what is a 'spouse of long standing' in nine letters? A stalemate!

It is currently the fashion in newspapers and magazines to include a pun or an allusion in the titles of articles, other than those reporting tragic news. For example, an article on environmental problems on Mount Kilimanjaro was headed *The Woes of Kilimanjaro*, playing on Ernest Hemingway's *The Snows of Kilimanjaro*. Some of these allusions can be quite clever. A Melbourne newspaper reported a bid for the leadership of a political party by a Senator Natasha Stott-Despoya with the title *Et tu, Natasha?* Readers of Shakespeare's *Julius Caesar* will recall that Caesar's friend, Brutus, is the last of the assassins to stab him, and Caesar asks *Et tu, Brute?* 'Even you, Brutus?' The paper's allusion to Shakespeare's play cleverly implied that the senator was being a traitor to her leader, without actually saying so. Allusions are a kind of secret communication between the author and part of the audience. Only those in the know get the allusion.

And so to conclude. While it may be true that the basic function of language is to communicate and exchange information, it is obvious that a large part of language use goes beyond the plain, straight-out message. People are forever playing with words, and humour is a prominent part of this activity.

Notes and sources

Unless specified here, all the jokes and examples are either in general circulation or from the author's experience, which includes jokes supplied by acquaintances.
Full details of the works cited are given in the References.

p. x   Further information on the use of humour consultants is to be found in Gibson's article in *Humor*.

pp. 1–21   Classifications of jokes are to be found in Attardo, *Linguistic Theories of Humour*.

p. 10   The Woody Allen quote is from *The Complete Prose Works of Woody Allen*, p. 300.

p. 16   Numerous works on satire are available, including Feinberg, *Introduction to Satire*. Kitchin provides a very readable coverage of parody in *A Survey of Burlesque and Parody in English*, and Muecke does likewise for irony in *The Compass of Irony*.

p. 19   The example from Butler appears on p. 17 of Muecke.

p. 20   The quote from Sir Boyle Roche is from Shipley, *Playing with Words*, p. 24.

p. 28   Freud writes about self-deprecation in Jewish humour in *Jokes and Their Relation to the Unconscious*, p.673. See also Davies's article in *Humor*.

p. 31   Further information on humour in European history can be found in Bremmer and Roodenburg, *A Cultural History of Humour*.
The women-parking joke is quoted from Chiaro, *The Language of Jokes*, p.8.

pp. 34   There's a good collection of political jokes in Larsen, *Wit as Weapon*. Anti-Nazi jokes can be found in Hillenbrand, *Underground Humour in Nazi Germany 1933–1945*.

p. 38–40   The passages quoted from Freud are from *Jokes and Their Relation to the Unconscious*, p. 664.

p. 41   For an in-depth discussion of language taboo, see Allan and Burridge, *Forbidden Words: Taboo and the Censoring of Language*.

p. 50   In *The Cambridge Encyclopedia of the English Language*, p.179, David Crystal points out that 'Elementary, dear Watson' does not occur in any of Sir Arthur Conan Doyle's Sherlock Holmes novels, though it does appear in a film.

p. 63   The 'wellness potential' phrase is quoted in Allan and Burridge, *Euphemism and Dysphemism*, p.167, and was taken from the *Medical Observer* of 19 January 1990. This is a celebrated example also quoted in various other places.

p. 68   The sources for the quotes are as follows: Bergson, *Le Rire*, p. 120; Freud, *Jokes and Their Relation to the Unconscious*, p.623; Holmes, *The Autocrat of the Breakfast Table*, p.11; and Redfern, *Puns*, p.14.

pp. 121   The joke from Freud comes from *Jokes and Their Relation to the Unconscious*, pp. 639 and 667.

p. 122–3   The quotations from Lord Chesterfield, Marya Mannes, and Dorothy Parker are to be found in Tripp, *The International Thesaurus of Quotations*.

p. 133   Freudian slips are discussed in Freud, *Psychopathology of Everyday Life*, chapter 5.

p. 140   The information about the origin of *mondegreen* is from the Wikipedia entry on the internet.
    The Eastman quote is from *Enjoyment of Laughter*, p. 147.

p. 145   The examples from Billings are quoted in Crystal, *The Cambridge Encyclopedia of the English Language*, p. 84.

p. 152–3   The examples from politicians can be found in various sources including Parris and Mason, *Read My Lips;* Ward, *Foolish Words*; and various websites.

p. 158   For a discussion of 'Ride a cock-horse', see Iona and Peter Opie, *The Oxford Dictionary of Nursery Rhymes*, pp. 65–6.

p. 160   For 'Oranges and Lemons' see Iona and Peter Opie, *ibid.*, pp. 337–9, and a number of 'Oranges and Lemons' websites.

Children's rhymes can be found in Turner *et al.*, *Cinderella Dressed in Yella*.

p. 163   The Calverly poem is from *Verses and Translations*, p. 24. Comic alphabets are treated in Partridge, *Comic Alphabets*.

p. 164   The Ogden Nash poem is from his *Collected Verse, from 1929 On*.

References and further reading

Allan, Keith and Burridge, Kate. 1991. *Euphemism and Dysphemism*. Oxford: Oxford University Press.

Allan, Keith and Burridge, Kate. 2006. *Forbidden Words: Taboo and the Censoring of Language*. Cambridge: Cambridge University Press.

Allen, Woody. 1991. *The Complete Prose Works of Woody Allen*. New York: Wing Books.

Attardo, Salvatore. 1994. *Linguistic Theories of Humour*. Berlin: Mouton de Gruyter.

Bergson, Henri. 1900. *Le Rire*. Paris. [*Laughter: An Essay on the Meaning of the Comic*. Authorized translation by Cloudesley Brereton. 1912. New York: Macmillan.]

Blair, W. and Hill, H. 1978. *American Humor*. New York: Oxford University Press.

Bremmer, Jan and Roodenburg, Herman (eds). 1997. *A Cultural History of Humour*. Cambridge: Polity Press.

Burridge, Kate. 2002. *Blooming English*. Sydney: ABC Books.

Calverley, Charles Stuart. 1881. *Verses and Translations by C.S.C.* Cambridge: Deighton, Bell [first published 1862].

Chiaro, Delia. 1992. *The Language of Jokes: Analysing Verbal Play*. London: Routledge.

Cohen, Ted. 1999. *Jokes: Philosophical Thoughts on Joking Matters*. Chicago: University of Chicago Press.

Crystal, David. 1995. *The Cambridge Encyclopedia of the English Language*. Cambridge: Cambridge University Press.

Crystal, David. 1998. *Language Play*. London: Penguin.

Davies, Christie. 1991. Exploring the thesis of the self-deprecating Jewish sense of humor. *Humor* 4: 189–209.

Eastman, Max. 1937. *Enjoyment of Laughter*. London: Hamish Hamilton.

Espy, Willard R. 1972. *The Game of Words*. New York: Bramhall House.

Feinberg, Leonard. 1967. *Introduction to Satire*. Ames: Iowa State University Press.

Freud, Sigmund. 1901. *Psychopathology of Everyday Life*. [Brill, A. A. 1995. *The Basic Writings of Sigmund Freud*. New York: The Modern Library. *Psychopathology* occupies pp. 1–117 and references in the text are to this translation.]

Freud, Sigmund. 1905. *Witz und seine Beziehung zum Unbewussten [Jokes and Their Relation to the Unconscious]*. Leipzig: Deuticke. [Brill, A. A. 1995. *The Basic Writings of Sigmund Freud*. New York: The Modern Library. *Jokes* occupies pp. 601–771 and references in the text are to this translation.]

Gibson, Donald E. 1994. Humor consulting: laughs for power and profit in organizations. *Humor* 7: 403–28.

Glenn, Phillip. 2003. *Laughter in Interaction*. Cambridge: Cambridge University Press.

Goldstein, Laurence. 1990. The linguistic interest of verbal humour. *Humor* 3: 37–52.

Hillenbrand, F. K. M. 1995. *Underground Humour in Nazi Germany 1933–1945*. London: Routledge.

Holmes, Oliver Wendell. 1891. *The Autocrat of the Breakfast Table*. London: Sampson Low.

Hughes, P. and Hammond, P. 1978. *Upon the Pun*. London: Allen.

Kitchin, George. 1931. *A Survey of Burlesque and Parody in English*. New York: Russell & Russell.

Labov, William. 1972. *Language in the Inner City*. Philadelphia: University of Pennsylvania Press.

Larsen, Egon. 1980. *Wit as Weapon: The Political Joke in History*. London: Frederick Muller.

Lauder, Afferbeck. 1965. *Let Stalk Strine*. Sydney: Ure Smith.

Lauder, Afferbeck. 1968. *Fraffly Well Spoken: How to Speak the Language of London's West End*. Sydney: Ure Smith.

McGhee, Paul E. 1979. *Humor: Its Origin and Development*. San Francisco: W. H. Freeman.

McGhee, Paul E. and Goldstein, Jeffrey H. 1983. *Handbook of Humor Research*. New York: Springer-Verlag.

Morreall, John. 1983. *Taking Laughter Seriously*. Albany: State University of New York Press.

Muecke, D. C. 1969. *The Compass of Irony*. London: Methuen.

Mulkay, M. J. 1988. *On Humour: Its Nature and Its Place in Modern Society*. Cambridge: Polity Press.

Nash, Ogden. 1961. *Collected Verse, from 1929 On*. London: J. M. Dent.

Nash, Walter. 1985. *The Language of Humour: Style and Technique in Comic Discourse*. London: Longman.

Opie, Iona and Opie, Peter (eds). 1952. *The Oxford Dictionary of Nursery Rhymes*. Oxford: Clarendon Press.

Parris, Matthew and Mason, Phil. 1997. *Read My Lips: A Treasury of the Things Politicians Wish They Hadn't Said*. London: Penguin.

Partridge, Eric. 1961. *Comic Alphabets: Their Origin, Development, Nature*, with drawings by Michael Foreman. London : Routledge & Kegan Paul.

Raskin, Victor. 1985. *Semantic Mechanisms of Humour*. Dordrecht: Reidel.

Redfern, Walter. 1984. *Puns*. Oxford: Blackwell in association with André Deutsch.

Shipley, Joseph T. 1960. *Playing with Words*. Englewood Cliffs, NJ: Prentice-Hall.

Tripp, Rhoda Thomas. 1976. *The International Thesaurus of Quotations*. Harmondsworth: Penguin.

Turner, Ian, Factor, June and Lowenstein, Wendy (eds). 1978. *Cinderella Dressed in Yella*. Richmond (Vic.): Heinemann Educational.

Ward, Laura. 2003. *Foolish Words*. London and New York: Viking Publishing (Penguin).

Wilkes, G. A. 1990. *A Dictionary of Australian Colloquialisms*. 3rd edn. Sydney: Sydney University Press in conjunction with Oxford University Press [first edition 1978].

Wilson, Christopher P. 1979. *Jokes: Form, Content, Use and Function*. London: Academic Press.

Index

Printed in the United States
202379BV00002B/1-51/A

9 781845 533304